KW-224-003

GLOBAL PRIVATIZATION AND ITS IMPACT

INGRID J. HAGEN

AND

THEA S. HALVORSEN

EDITORS

Nova Science Publishers, Inc.

New York

UCB
176634

Copyright © 2009 by Nova Science Publishers, Inc.

All rights reserved. No part of this book may be reproduced, stored in a retrieval system or transmitted in any form or by any means: electronic, electrostatic, magnetic, tape, mechanical photocopying, recording or otherwise without the written permission of the Publisher.

For permission to use material from this book please contact us:
Telephone 631-231-7269; Fax 631-231-8175
Web Site: http://www.novapublishers.com

NOTICE TO THE READER

The Publisher has taken reasonable care in the preparation of this book, but makes no expressed or implied warranty of any kind and assumes no responsibility for any errors or omissions. No liability is assumed for incidental or consequential damages in connection with or arising out of information contained in this book. The Publisher shall not be liable for any special, consequential, or exemplary damages resulting, in whole or in part, from the readers' use of, or reliance upon, this material. Any parts of this book based on government reports are so indicated and copyright is claimed for those parts to the extent applicable to compilations of such works.

Independent verification should be sought for any data, advice or recommendations contained in this book. In addition, no responsibility is assumed by the publisher for any injury and/or damage to persons or property arising from any methods, products, instructions, ideas or otherwise contained in this publication.

This publication is designed to provide accurate and authoritative information with regard to the subject matter covered herein. It is sold with the clear understanding that the Publisher is not engaged in rendering legal or any other professional services. If legal or any other expert assistance is required, the services of a competent person should be sought. FROM A DECLARATION OF PARTICIPANTS JOINTLY ADOPTED BY A COMMITTEE OF THE AMERICAN BAR ASSOCIATION AND A COMMITTEE OF PUBLISHERS.

LIBRARY OF CONGRESS CATALOGING-IN-PUBLICATION DATA

Global privatization and its impact / Ingrid J. Hagen and Thea S. Halvorsen (editors).
   p. cm.
  ISBN 978-1-60456-785-4 (hardcover)
  1. Privatization. 2. Economic policy. 3. International economic relations. 4. Competition. 5. Globalization--Economic aspects. I. Hagen, Ingrid J. II. Halvorsen, Thea S.
  HD3850.G56 2009
  338.9'25--dc22
          2008037514

Published by Nova Science Publishers, Inc. ✦ New York

GLOBAL PRIVATIZATION
AND ITS IMPACT

176634

£74.50

CONTENTS

PREFACE

In recent years, the economic policy of privatization, which is defined as the transfer of property or responsibility from public sector to private sector, is one of the global phenomenon that increases use of markets to allocate resources. One important motivation for privatization is to help develop factor and product markets, as well as security markets. Progress in privatization is correlated with improvements in perceived political and investment risk. Many emerging countries have gradually reduced their political risks during the course of sustained privatization. In fact, most risk resolution seems to take place as privatization proceeds to its later stage. Alternative benefits of privatization are improved risk sharing and increased liquidity and activity of the market. One of the main methods to develop privatization is entering a new stock to the markets for arising competition. This book provides leading edge research on this field from around the globe.

Healthiness is something which mankind has seemingly always striven to maintain. Ill health challenges our religious and logical attitude to life itself and has generated a quest for that elusive elixir. Knowledge relating to healthcare has come at a price which has been fiercely guarded by those who appear to possess it. However, knowledge is a relative commodity and changes with time as our interpretation of the forces of nature become more robust. When we try to apply a humanitarian approach to healthcare we are confronted with balancing good and evil knowing that mankind is not innately endowed with infinite generosity towards his neighbour. The conflict between the *haves* and the *have-nots* has generated an uneasy relationship between the charitable or public providers of healthcare and private enterprise.

In Chapter 1 the author concentrates mainly on how a nationalised public hospital service has found itself in conflict with private enterprise.

In Chapter 2 we take stock of the performance of share issue privatizations in Australia and find that consistent with our conjecture that investors expected the privatization to significantly impact on industry counterparts through industrial repositioning, the industry counterparts reacted negatively to the privatization announcements. In the long term, the privatized firms outperformed the market index and the industry counterparts. We also find that the firms privatized by the Federal (Commonwealth) Government had significant market impact than those privatized by State Governments. In terms of operating performance, we observe that the privatized firms have become more profitable in the post privatization period than in the pre privatization period, but their operating efficiency has not significantly improved. The privatization has also led to a significant attrition in staff levels, especially in the years immediately following the year of privatization. Our results show that after controlling for contemporaneous economy-wide factors, share issue privatization has yielded significant stock market and operating performance improvements for privatized firms in Australia.

The liberalization of the land use market has become the most pressing economic issue for the Chinese Government in recent years. The objective of this paper is to provide an overview of land market operations in China with an update of its land policies. It will first present some background information about the establishment of the land market and its transformation, and then document the land development process in China. The foregoing section discusses the problems associated with land acquisitions and how the Chinese Government has tried to overcome them, especially the loss of agricultural land due to its conversion from agricultural to non-agricultural uses, and the disputes between farmers and governments. The last section will offer a summary of Chapter 3.

In the 1980's, the discussions and applications of privatization which began in England are still going ahead increasingly for many developed and developing countries from the beginning of 1990. Recently, privatization turned into a strategy which is preferred by developing countries for solving major economic problems or which is imposed to these countries by international organizations. It seems that the discussions about this subject are going to maintain its importance for the next years.

In Chapter 4, it is aimed to construct policy suggestions about how to pass from power doctrine to welfare doctrine according to privatization applications considering threats and opportunities of globalization in developing countries. Moreover, in the scope of privatization policies, dynamics of transiting from populist-voluntarist economy management to economic democracy is going to be discussed and a regulation model which can be taken as a guide for policy-makers in developing countries is going to be created based on the case of Turkey. In short, new policy suggestions are tried to be developed relating to privatization applications.

As explained in Chapter 5, the world-wide privatization and liberalization of energy sectors have been one of the contemporary exhibitions of permanent "primitive accumulation" process. Apart from varieties displayed by various countries in their liberalization and privatization experiences, all these experiences have displayed some common characteristics: privatization by force, blackmail, fraud and corruption. These common characteristics have been central to the so-called "primitive accumulation" process. This process, inherently, has ended up losers (reforming countries, governments, households...etc.) and also winners (international energy firms, privatization consultancy firms, capital as whole...etc.).

Breeding companies need some form of legal or biological protection measures to assure revenues from genetic improvement and investment in genetic material. Fish farmers and fish breeders need access to genetic resources for food production and further development and sustainable use of fish genetic material. The objective of Chapter 6 is to discuss the international and domestic legal processes and the needs of fish breeders in the aquaculture sector. For this we will review:

1.   The rationale for ensuring access to and for using legal measures for protection of breeding materials in aquaculture

2.   A Norwegian case on Norwegian salmon breeding and farming, where three dimensions that may affect choices of protection and the scope for access to fish genetic resources are considered: Awareness among fish breeders of international regulations of

genetic resources; evolving structures within the aquaculture sector; technological developments and biological features presenting options and barriers

3.   The options available for protection of aquaculture genetic resources in both developed and developing countries.

As explained in Chapter 7, in recent years, the economic policy of privatization, which is defined as the transfer of property or responsibility from public sector to private sector, is one of the global phenomena that increases use of markets to allocate resources. One important motivation for privatization is to help develop factor and product markets, as well as security markets. Progress in privatization is correlated with improvements in perceived political and investment risk. Many emerging countries have gradually reduced their political risks during the course of sustained privatization. In fact, most risk resolution seems to take place as privatization proceeds to its later stage. Alternative benefits of privatization are improved risk sharing and increased liquidity and activity of the market. One of the main methods to develop privatization is entering a new stock to the markets for arising competition. However, attention to the capability of the markets to accept a new stock is substantial. Without considering the above statement, it is possible to reduce the market's efficiency. In other words, introduction of a new stock to the market usually decreases the stage of development and activity and increases the risk. Based on complexity theory, we quantify how the following factors: stage of development, activity, risk and investment horizons play roles in the privatization.

In: Global Privatization and Its Impact
Editors: I.J. Hagen and T.S. Halvorsen, pp. 1-25
ISBN: 978-1-60456-785-4
© 2008 Nova Science Publishers, Inc.

Chapter 1

HEALTHCARE'S UNHEALTHY ASSOCIATION WITH THE MARKETPLACE

Mark Aitken
Colchester General Hospital, Colchester, Essex, UK

Introduction

Healthiness is something which mankind has seemingly always striven to maintain. Ill health challenges our religious and logical attitude to life itself and has generated a quest for that elusive elixir. Knowledge relating to healthcare has come at a price which has been fiercely guarded by those who appear to possess it. However, knowledge is a relative commodity and changes with time as our interpretation of the forces of nature become more robust. When we try to apply a humanitarian approach to healthcare we are confronted with balancing good and evil knowing that mankind is not innately endowed with infinite generosity towards his neighbour. The conflict between the *haves* and the *have-nots* has generated an uneasy relationship between the charitable or public providers of healthcare and private enterprise.

Any partnership between the public and private delivery of healthcare has to be uncompromisingly transparent and accept that the patient's welfare is paramount. In reality this relationship, particularly in the United Kingdom (UK), is flawed since it is driven by profit and lacks honest accountability.

Politicians realise that, with all the advances in technology and pharmaceutical inventiveness, providing an even-handed service for everyone can only be sustained by increased taxation. However, increased taxation puts in jeopardy the politician's desire to remain in power and therefore a complicated web of deception is needed in order to allay the suspicions of the population.

In industry production targets keep companies focussed on profitability. Conversely healthcare targets are focussed on political popularity. Target setting merely moves the goal posts. When the budget is fixed enhancement of the service in one area leads to degradation in other areas. Concealing the downside of these moves is the politicians' forte.

In recent times several measures have been introduced in order facilitate this political agenda. These have included National Health Service (NHS) Direct call centres, Private

Finance Initiatives to bank roll new hospital buildings, Independent Sector Treatment Centres to take patients off NHS waiting lists and new remuneration formulae for hospitals based on a capped Payment by Results strategy.

Sadly the medical profession has failed to recognise the subtlety and potential destructiveness of these measures either because of personal conflicts of interest or sheer boredom with the repeated political tinkering with the system which has compromised their ability to deliver an equitable service.

In this article I shall concentrate mainly on how a nationalised public hospital service has found itself in conflict with private enterprise.

The Nature of The Problem

Whoever pays the piper calls the tune. But who is calling whom and what are the tunes? In the realms of healthcare the purse strings are held either by private financial institutions or the political masters of the critical population. Neither has the knowledge base to deliver the goods but do have the skills to manipulate the providers and recipients to support their individual strategies. At the end of the day it is the recipients of healthcare who pay the piper either in the form of insurance premiums, taxes or devolved spiritual ennoblement. Nonetheless, in most societies it is the insurance companies and the politicians who decide what the recipient can receive, driven as they are by their own agendas, profit and political posturing, respectively.

Historically healthcare was related to the alleviation of suffering. Recovery from disease was left in the lap of the gods. Today, with the impact of science and pseudo-science on healthcare, the emphasis has shifted to the perpetuation of life. Paradoxically those institutions which have been set up specifically to alleviate suffering, such as the Macmillan Foundation, receive most of their funding from charitable sources and not from the public purse. Clearly the healthcare bureaucracy does not now appear to rate the alleviation of suffering very highly.

The vision of providing universal healthcare is looking into a bottomless pit of disease. Therefore it is necessary either to find an inexhaustible source of revenue or to limit the scope of health management. Since there is no pot of gold, rationing the service is unavoidable. How do you ration something which is almost as complicated as the human genome and how do you obfuscate "rationing" without alienating those to whom the service is being offered?

Who should make the decisions on disease management? Would we have more trust in the judgement of the politicians who raise and spend our taxes or the leaders of our various religions? Politicians and religious leaders exert power over their people, albeit in different ways. Would we be comfortable to put our health in the hands of those driven by political or religious fervour and confer to them the power over life and death? Would we prefer to trust the decisions of the medical profession? Doctors have the knowledge and training to know what might be "best" for the individual patient. In all events we would want to be assured that those involved in our healthcare would not stand to profit from our misfortunes. Where there is a sacred cow there will always be someone prepared to put their hands to milking it.

Private healthcare, which has always been available for the wealthy, is invariably driven by profitability. The private hospitals and clinics were built to a specification best able to select those parts of the healthcare menu which had the greatest potential for profit. Public healthcare is not afforded that luxury and is unable to choose their clientele or their patients' disease profile. Here the quality and quantity of service deliverable is wholly dependent upon the supply of public funds. Balancing supply and demand is challenging. The unwary can be lured into the pursuit of a holy grail that beckons but defies capture. Administrators require absolute even-handedness and infinite wisdom. Wisdom being the synthesis of knowledge and time may be lacking at the inception of this process. However, provided that knowledge gained is converted into wisdom then real progress can be made. With a politically driven health service, such as the NHS, the politicians and managers, who are in post for relatively short periods of time, spend much of that time trying to reinvent the wheel instead of concentrating on the construction and performance of the vehicle. At the end of the day the wheel is still a disc and not a polygon but time and money have been wasted proving what should have been obvious from the start. These political foibles then become dressed up in the clothes of apparent success as one swathe of administrators give way to the next group of ne'er-do-wells.

In regard to the delivery of healthcare there has always been a dichotomy between those who seek to profit from the misfortunes of others and those whose ministrations to the sick are wholly humanitarian and without financial implications. Clearly the spectrum between these two extremes is considerable and often conceals conflicts of interest exhibited by staff who have the freedom to exploit both the patient and the source of funding. Being found with your hand in the cookie jar is not necessarily seen as a professional indiscretion. The medical profession is often seen as defenders of their personal wealth rather than as champions of better services for patients. Efforts to introduce legislation to deliver operational transparency have been half hearted and are likely to be thwarted for the foreseeable future unless all parties re-examine their contribution to the prioritisation of the service. Because these conflicts have not been resolved the humanitarian aspirations of the NHS are frequently sidelined and substituted by a game of political football.

The UK Experience of Nationalised Healthcare

In order to understand the complexity of the NHS it might be helpful to examine its *raison d'être* and to see how this has been corrupted by the subsequent perpetual motion of the goal posts.

Aneurin (Nye) Bevan, the Minister for Health in 1948, had a vision that if the underprivileged, and in particular the mining communities in South Wales, had free access to healthcare, then within a generation the cost of providing healthcare would diminish. A noble gesture but not based on sound evidence and as with most adventures into the unknown the devil was in the detail. Nye was hell bent on pushing through the necessary legislation at any price and had the political backing of a huge parliamentary socialist majority. The medical profession was represented by Lord Moran (Charles Wilson) who wasn't nicknamed *"Corkscrew Charlie"* because of an affiliation to alcohol. He had been Winston Churchill's personal physician for many years and was also the President of the Royal College of Physicians from 1940 to 1951. When a political evangelist negotiates with an uncompromising representative of a lukewarm profession, deals are likely to be made which reward both parties but which compromise the long term interests of patients.

The deal gave the hospital Consultants a very generous salary for services to the NHS whilst allowing them to continue to enjoy the luxuries of private practice and retain control of a system of "meritorious" awards.

By 1951 the Labour Party could see the red light of economical insolvency looming up ahead and introduced charges for false teeth and spectacles and a one shilling (£0.05) prescription charge. This action gutted Nye Bevan although he did reluctantly admit that the population was "*swallowing gallons of free medicine and not even returning the empty bottles!*"

Prior to the introduction of the NHS medical fees were discretionary. The cost of running hospitals, including the payment of staff, was almost wholly dependant upon charitable donations. Hospital consultants relied upon private practice to give them a reasonable standard of living. For some that standard of living was more reasonable than others. General Practitioners (GPs) owned the premises from which they practised and were paid directly by their patients for services rendered.

After the birth of the NHS the GPs retained ownership of their surgeries but their remuneration became a salaried service relating to the number of patients registered with them and not the actual services rendered.

In the hospital service the implementation of the NHS involved the nationalisation of hospital buildings and land, and the allocation of funds to pay for the day to day expense of procuring consumables, buildings maintenance and the payment of staff. The buildings and land had usually been owned and managed by local borough councils often having previously been bequeathed by generous entrepreneurs. In some cases these fortunes had been amassed by usurping their workforce. Donating some of their wealth to charity may have been motivated by a desire to earn themselves a place in the afterlife. Later, with rationalisation of the built environment, swathes of hospital property were sold off, but the charity for which the money/property had originally been donated was often sidelined in order to use the proceeds for personal and more politically expedient issues instead of reinvesting the proceeds, with appropriate enhancements, to modernise the remaining local hospital infrastructure. Simply, asset stripping.

The remuneration of Consultants in the hospital service remained a two tiered system but there was the option to be a full time employee of the NHS with a very attractive salary. Even those who retained part time NHS status received a substantial salary compared with the previous pittance for attending to hospital patients. For them private practice became the icing on the cake. This part-time arrangement with the NHS was especially favourable to surgeons who could earn several times their NHS salary in the private sector.

Junior doctors were wholly salaried and their remuneration had little reference to their conditions of service or the hours worked. Deductions were made for accommodation and meals. This non consultant workforce powered the NHS. Its members were largely uncomplaining except when it came to the quality of accommodation and meals. They laboured in the hope that after many years of dedicated service, the attainment of specific postgraduate qualifications and blessed with impeccable references they would attain Consultant status. It was a workforce that was easy to exploit.

The hospitals had to provide a large number of in house facilities in addition to direct healthcare. These included the management of staff accommodation, laundry, cleaning, catering and car parking. Later the franchises for these services were selectively sold off to facilities management companies that claimed to be able to offer the same service at a lower cost and still make a profit for their share holders. In some instances these delegated services included laboratory and imaging facilities. The NHS lacked the foresight to give their staff the opportunity to learn the skills to run these services more cost effectively, preferring instead to divert public money into the private sector. Unfortunately the hospitals were still required to employ staff to enforce these private contracts and monitor the quality of service provided.

Previously, self regulation had been the preferred method for monitoring the quality of the service delivered. Spot visits by senior members of staff, such as the Matron, kept people on their toes and discouraged complacency. Now this has been replaced by a layer of middle managers who push around paper trails of statistical benchmarks shrouded in mumbo jumbo which can be massaged according to the theme of the day in order to deliver any particular aspect of managerial self gratification.

Standards of Care and Hospital Infrastructure

At the inception of the NHS the condition of the fabric of the compulsorily acquired hospital buildings was very variable. Some hospitals were furbished generously. Others were relatively dilapidated. Many prefabricated hospital buildings had been erected to take casualties from the Second World War and by 1948 were predominantly serving the civilian population. Although inpatient facilities were rudimentary, the staff paid great attention to ensuring that patient dignity and privacy were preserved. Patients in wards were segregated by gender with appropriate toileting facilities. Each ward housed up to about 30 patients with the beds arranged around the walls. These wards were called Nightingale wards. Mobile screens or curtains provided some privacy. It was uncommon for a ward to have more than two side rooms and these were reserved for critical cases which had been so designated by the ward sister. The ward sister also arranged the location of each patient in the ward according to sensitivity and nursing requirements. Visiting was strictly controlled and rarely exceeded an hour each day. Doctors' ward rounds and the provision of nursing care took precedence over visiting. Disturbances at night were difficult to eliminate and in order to ensure a reasonable duration of sleep night sedation was the rule and barbiturates became increasingly the drug of choice in the 1950s.

In the private sector hospital accommodation was very different and in principle has changed little over the last 60 years. Essentially each patient had their own private room with personal toileting facilities and relatively open visiting hours. Night sedation was less often required. The size and splendour of private accommodation within NHS hospitals was often rudimentary. It was not surprising therefore that entrepreneurs saw this deficiency in the fabric of the NHS as an exploitable opportunity. Gradually more and more private hospitals were built. Profitability was proportional to bed occupancy and the rapidity with which patients could be turned around (i.e. length of stay). The private sector realised from the start that the cream of profitability came from treating patients requiring simple operative procedures with predictable turn around times. Emergency patients were carefully scrutinised before allowing admission because the unpredictable variability of outcome posed the greatest challenge to maintaining their planned patient throughput. The medical staffing of private hospitals was profoundly inferior to that afforded to NHS patients but the risk to the patient was small because their selection criteria. However, few if any patients entering these private establishments were made aware of the fact that in an emergency their chances of survival would be inferior to that afforded to patients in a NHS hospital.

Addressing the limitations of providing dignity and privacy within NHS hospitals was a challenge which successive administrations have tried to avoid but where attempts were made to deliver equity the compromises involved were not publicised. The ultimate goal would have been the provision of single room accommodation for all NHS patients. This would have involved a several fold increase in the footprint of all inpatient accommodation as well as an escalation of medical and nursing staff costs because the limited ability to observe patients in single rooms requires more staff than would be required for a classical Nightingale ward. Clearly no administration was going to underwrite such an ambitious scheme let alone the faltering economy of post war Britain. Consequently we have seen a succession of politically motivated compromises which have given priority to financial solvency and paid lip service to patient dignity and privacy.

Rationalisation of the built environment meant the centralisation of services and closure of smaller satellite hospitals. In terms of providing appropriate cover for medical emergencies this made good sense although outpatients and hospital visitors might have to travel longer distances. The administration saw hospital closures and the sale of their assets and land as good financial management. This was accompanied by a modest increase in single rooms and wards divided into small bays suitable for single sex accommodation. Unfortunately the plan could evolve in several stages with a planned reduction of bed numbers resulting in increased bed occupancy and designated single sex bays and their toileting facilities becoming unisex. Patient dignity and privacy was the first casualty of these bean counting exercises.

Changing the Built Environment of Hospitals

Hospital buildings tie up large amounts of capital but have little market value because of their highly specialised usage. Whereas property in the domestic housing market undergoes continuous appreciation hospital buildings represent a wasting asset. This paradox is currently being approached in two very different ways.

Firstly one can buy or hire cheap prefabricated temporary buildings. These are usually erected as single or two storey extensions to permanent buildings. The downside is that collectively they occupy a relatively large footprint and limit the scope for future permanent developments. Connectivity to the main built environment is rarely ideal. Many of their internal walls are load-bearing thereby making internal alterations to accommodate changes in function difficult or impossible.

Secondly one can pass on the risk involved in major capital developments by inviting the private sector to build and maintain them. It was with this in mind that the Private Finance Initiative (PFI) approach was spawned.

The Private Finance Initiative Approach

Until the 1990s hospital building and rebuilding was funded by Treasury capital. The Hospital Trust then paid the Treasury an annual capital charge, intended to reflect the market value of the property. It was a type of mortgage but without a finite date for closure.

The Treasury's alternative approach was to devise a funding mechanism which would no longer appear as a debt incurred by the public purse because the capital raised for PFI schemes would come from the private sector.

The Ministry of Defence (MOD) used this facility to bankroll the building of improved accommodation for servicemen. It gave credibility to the concept that when off the battlefield a soldier should enjoy some dignity and privacy. There was no expectation of improved productivity. However repayments to the private consortia would eat into the budget for purchasing military hardware and therefore in theory limit military effectiveness.

State school building projects embarked on this initiative only to find that maintenance contracts were frequently sold on by the consortia to operatives who did not appear to be bound by the initial contract. New school buildings might improve the environment for teachers and pupils and enhance the teaching process but at the expense of the budget for books and stationery and other essential educational aids because there was no commensurate increase in capitation fees to meet the capital repayments to the private consortia.

In regard to healthcare the PFI process was probably more convoluted than in other public services. Nonetheless it was well structured and carefully regulated. The procedure would start with the Hospital Trust identifying a clinical need and a feasible economical clinical solution. This Outline Building Strategy had to be approved by the local Strategic Health Authority and then presented to the Secretary of State for Health for ministerial approval. Once outline approval had been granted the Hospital Trust had to develop a detailed Outline Building Case (OBC) which laid out the overall benefits to the community and showed how in general terms an affordable solution would be delivered. This process, funded by a grant from the Department of Health (DoH), allowed the Trust to appoint a Project Team that would carry out the various stages required up to the signing of a definitive contract with a private finance consortium. The project would be advertised, bids would be tendered, and eventually a preferred bidder would be appointed to develop the project to a point where all parties could agree both the structural and functional solution and the affordability. Throughout this exercise representatives from the Office of Government Commerce (OGC) Gateway Process would visit the Hospital Trust at regular intervals in order to interview the Project Team and the Chief Executive. Their progress reports would identify problems, offer solutions and where appropriate commended the Project Team on their work.

The PFI process sounds pretty straight forward and appears to carry an assumed guarantee that eventually the project will be signed off, and the building will be completed, commissioned and opened to deliver a better service for patients. Unfortunately in the NHS nothing is cast in stone. Aspirations change. Technology becomes more costly. People come out of the woodwork to challenge the solution already agreed with the preferred bidder. The Primary Care Trust (PCT), currently the budget holder at a local level, introduces conditions regarding the delivery of care which challenge the functionality and affordability of the project. The project team starts to cut out those parts of the project which are perceived to be providing staff with a better work environment in order to retain the enhancement of patient care. Compromises are made with the Borough Council because site accessibility for patients and emergencies carries a lower priority than the local traffic plan. Eventually even patient services are trimmed in order to comply with new political directives such as the introduction of Payment by Results (PbR), the hitting of new waiting time targets, and the development of Independent Sector Treatment Centres (ISTCs). A project which starts as a service for patients finishes up in a financially driven political no mans land.

An Alternative Strategy

Private schools (paradoxically termed Public Schools) and University Colleges have historically obtained capital for improving their built environment by inviting former students and local industry to make charitable donations. In effect these were one-off donations which funded tangible structures which the donors could see and be proud of. Without such a mechanism the only alternative to enhancing the built environment would have been to raise the fees paid by current students. The latter strategy carried the risk that fewer students might enrol with a consequent fall in revenue and possible closure of the school.

In industry capital investment is aimed at increasing productivity. For the MOD, state schools and in particular public healthcare, the provider currently has neither the control over the demand for the service nor the guarantee of appropriate and commensurate remuneration for services rendered.

In the private sector this impasse would not come about because the built environment is the main attraction for their potential clientele. The high capital investment in that built environment is recouped by sweating the resource without any risk to patient safety. This is not achievable in the public sector because without single room accommodation for all patients, irrespective of clinical need, increasing bed occupancy beyond 85% is likely to lead to an increased risk of spreading infection and a deterioration in the quality of the service deliverable. Having to release ones emotions or bodily functions in a public arena will cause personal distress and a mixture of stress, annoyance, embarrassment, disgust and fear in ones neighbours. The application of standards of dignity and privacy to hospital construction should therefore be aimed at avoiding these unpleasant experiences for patients.

The most appropriate solution in a nationalised health service where the government ministers claim that they really are "putting patients first" is for them to agree that enhancements in the built environment of hospitals which address patient dignity and privacy should be taken out of any private financial package and paid for up front by the Treasury. Such a declaration of intent should not be permitted to alter as political parties change places and ministers play musical chairs. The standard of accommodation espoused by NHS Estates (a quango within a quango) is rarely available today except in recently built or comprehensively reengineered wards. Their recommendations include four bedded bays with en suite toileting facilities and an increase in the proportion of single rooms to 30% of the total available beds. This declaration should define the gold standard imposed on hospital construction, along with adequate backup and flexibility to cope with major disasters and epidemics.

At the present time the DoH, appears to be condoning the poor built environment of many hospitals instead of encouraging the attainment of the standards set by NHS Estates. Hospital infrastructure needs to be modernised and the capital to bankroll this initiative has to be funded centrally without jeopardising the Hospital Trust's income trail. This could be achieved, without the politicians losing of face, if the DoH agreed to fund directly those elements of any new build which specifically addressed patient dignity and privacy.

Changing the Hospital Service Profile

In the UK during the last decade there have been a number of politically motivated initiatives intended to increase access to treatment and improve the patient experience. These have been driven by targets and partially funded by tapping into alternative sources of capital. There was however a more sinister agenda alluded to by Tony Blair (the outgoing Prime Minister) in a television documentary made after he had left office. The thrust of his argument was that, following their appointment, senior hospital staff and GPs effectively inherit a job for life and that this state of affairs presents an obstacle to changing working practices and was likely to make the Labour party's task of NHS reform an uphill struggle. Thereafter subtle changes to Consultant and GP contracts were engineered in return for a modest increase in salary. The contracts gave Hospital Trusts and Primary Care Trusts greater powers to implement political, as opposed to clinical, targets and reforms. The innuendo which drove these changes forward was more likely to alienate the profession than confer ownership. Ownership is an essential part of any reform.

The Target Driven Work Ethic

Politicians are always on the lookout for aspirations which bolster their image. First identify and then exaggerate a defect in functional performance. Then set an easy but arbitrary performance target and reward those who achieve it. Finally crank up the performance target, redefine it as a performance standard and penalise institutions that fail to achieve it. In industry performance targets are driven by survival or greed.

1. Targets may help a failing company to galvanise its workforce to achieve greater productivity in order to remain solvent and thereby continue to provide a source of employment. This tactic works for small family businesses where there are strong bonds between management and the workforce. Even austere measures are seen as an interim strategy whilst everyone works and thinks together to derive a more cost effective way of improving productivity.

2. In the other scenario targets are used to boost productivity by paying workers performance related bonuses. This might take the form of working longer hours and thereby sweating the resource or by increasing the hourly output of each employee by paying them for piecework. Here the emphasis is on getting a foothold on the upward spiral of incremental growth where increasing the company's share of the market leads to greater profits, more capital for reinvestment, improved technology, squeezing out competition, greater profits, *etc., etc.*

In healthcare performance targets appear at first sight to be altruistic when in reality they are designed as cost effective solutions to problems which more often than not have been poorly researched.

The application of this sort of work ethic does not sit comfortably in public healthcare where attention has historically been focussed on clinical need and not on patients past the post.

A&E Waiting Times

The political initiative to introduce Accident & Emergency (A&E) waiting time targets had been precipitated by graphic complaints of patients abandoned on trolleys in A&E corridors for hours and in some instances days before being transferred to a bed or the mortuary. The politicians, with a characteristic disingenuous gesture, assumed that the doctors and nurses had lost the plot when in fact these events were the inevitable consequence of the continuing reduction in the number of hospital beds weighed against an increased demand for emergency management resulting from curtailing GP out of hours services, the closure of community care homes, and waves of the worried well responding to the gratuitous but deadly forebodings of undiagnosed serious disease promulgated by the media. Thus worried patients or their carers, finding themselves unable to access their GP for help or reassurance in regard to a perceived emergency, take themselves off to the nearest A&E Department.

The introduction of waiting time targets in A&E Departments was a surreptitiously disguised carrot which quickly became transformed into a punitive stick. Initially Hospital Trusts received financial rewards for achieving arbitrary waiting time targets. Later on, 98% compliance with a waiting time target of 4 hours before the patient had either to be discharged or admitted became mandatory. Hospital Trusts failing to attain this target incurred penalties. The A&E Departments, finding themselves swamped with relatively trivial medical and social problems, were less able to give expeditious care to the more seriously sick patients who in turn might remain on a trolley in a hospital corridor for unacceptably long periods of time.

The politicians then compounded their initial error of judgement by introducing NHS Direct – a call centre for patients or their carers to contact when worried – and Drop in Centres, staffed by specialist nurses, similar in training and experience to those in A&E Departments, but without laboratory or imaging backup, to see patients whose medical/social problems could not be resolved over the phone. In order to offset these capital programmes the tariff paid to Hospital Trusts for seeing patients with minor injuries or illnesses was reduced. This bizarre political move assumed that caring healthcare professionals working in A&E Departments would reject patients with minor injuries and illnesses and redirect them to the nearest Drop in Centre. Contrary to the wisdom of the politicians, the local population soon learnt that it was more expedient to attend the nearest A&E Department than to run the risk of being passed from Call Centre to Drop in Centre before eventually being referred to an A&E Department. Hence the original political initiative had been turned into a circular rearrangement of service provision, which alienated hospital A&E staff still duty bound to see all arrivals but overstretched and severely stressed in order to hit the waiting time targets. Unfortunately, with the emphasis on hitting waiting time targets, patients tended not to be prioritised according to the seriousness of their condition. It was easier to meet the 98% 4 hour waiting time standard by seeing a lot of patients with trivial conditions quickly whilst allowing a few more seriously ill or injured patients to breach the target.

Hospital Waiting Lists

When a doctor identifies a medical problem which requires a surgical procedure a decision is also made on the urgency with which that operation should be performed. Clearly there is a wide variation between life threatening conditions and conditions which cause some minor inconvenience or handicap. Urgent operations will be carried out within a few hours or days but the remainder will be placed on a waiting list. Those patients on the waiting list will have various degrees of prioritisation attached to their entry relating to the seriousness of their condition. It is inevitable therefore that patients with the least health challenging conditions will progress more slowly to the head of the list than those where the surgical problem is more disabling. In some surgical specialties the demand for certain procedures greatly outstrips the facilities available and patients may for example have to wait for as long as two years for a cataract extraction or a hip replacement.

This situation posed a challenge to the politicians who responded by setting maximum waiting time targets. The assumption of the politicians was that NHS surgeons were not focussed on the plight of patients sitting on waiting lists for what seemed to patients like an eternity. The reality was that the lack of physical resources and manpower was at the heart of the problem. The politicians highlighted differences in throughput between surgeons working in the same specialty but in different parts of the country and attributed the disparities found to a mixture of incompetence, laziness and a desire to maintain the status quo in order to fuel private practice. Some of these snide accusations may have applied in certain cases but generally speaking this was an unwarranted slur on the profession. Undeterred, the politicians set an eighteen week waiting time target for all surgical procedures except where cancer was the suspected diagnosis when the target was reduced to four weeks. The clock started to tick as soon as the patient was referred by their GP and stopped on the day the procedure was carried out.

Where these targets could be met without the investment in additional resources it proved that operational inefficiencies had been responsible for poor performance. This was rarely the whole explanation. In most cases increased surgical throughput might provide extra revenue to pay for consumables and staffing but this source of income would not pay for extra operating theatres or beds. Without this injection of money the additional resources required had to be diverted from other care packages or else added to cumulative debt.

Extra day surgery sessions could be set up at weekends but overheads were excessive because it required the use of agency nurses and enhanced payments to surgical staff.

Extra inpatient sessions were hampered by the uncertainty of a predictable availability of surgical beds. A temporary solution was to transfer some NHS surgery to the local private hospital or to transfer convalescent patients blocking surgical beds to the private sector for their continuing care. Either way this created negative equity.

The political answer to the unenthusiastic efforts of Hospital Trusts to hit waiting list targets was to introduce Independent Sector Treatment Centres (ISTCs).

Public Independent Sector Treatment Centres

This contradictory concept came out of the political pledge to reduce hospital waiting lists. However it was a publicly affordable project only if it allowed the relevant hospital services to be downsized appropriately. The latter was not alluded to in the public launch of this new venture.

There is no doubt that private healthcare provides a service which reduces the burden on the public purse. This would be quite significant in a predominantly affluent society where private insurance is affordable both during a person's working life and in old age. The latter proviso is important because at least 40% of the NHS budget is spent on the elderly population. It is no great surprise therefore that after the age of 65 health insurance premiums become increasingly restrictive and unaffordable for most people apart from the wealthy.

What do you do if you are a middle class elderly homeowner with a small pension but your eyesight is failing due to a cataract or your mobility is severely restricted because of an arthritic hip? Your expectation of life is shrinking. You are accelerating towards your final demise. A two year waiting time for surgery becomes unacceptably long. Serious consideration needs to be given to finding the capital for an expeditious private operation. Home owners might see the logic in re-mortgaging their home in order to release enough capital. Perhaps that is not so unreasonable. However, the politicians wishing to gain valuable brownie points at the ballot box, claimed that they could remove this personal financial burden by reducing waiting lists through the sponsorship of ISTCs. These centres would be built, commissioned and run by private consortia, but the work they performed on behalf of the NHS would be funded by the local PCT. However, the consortia backing ISTCs unsurprisingly would not take part in this initiative unless their income from the NHS was guaranteed and at an itemised cost of at least that offered to Hospital Trusts. Since the local PCT holds that budget, which has already been fixed by central government, the only way the PCT could find that money would be by imposing a levy on the local Hospital Trusts. Because the income generated by the Hospital Trusts had to come from items of service performed, the levy would become a millstone round their necks. Unless the Hospital Trust could reduce their operating costs to a level well below that incurred by the ISTC, they would fail to balance their books. The whole process then would become a downward spiral handicapping the functionality of the Hospital Trust. Short sighted local administrators failed to acknowledge this as a hidden *weapon of self destruction* of the NHS. No doubt the functionaries in the DoH just smiled inscrutably.

Interestingly the medical profession as a whole displayed an ambivalent attitude towards this plan. The Royal College of Physicians made it clear that they would support this innovation only where Hospital Trusts lacked the capacity to increase their level of activity in order to comply with new waiting list targets. The Royal College of Surgeons were more ambiguous, maybe because increased surgical activity outside NHS establishments would be likely to boost the income of surgeons and offset any loss of income from patients who would otherwise have opted for a privately funded operation.

If the DoH identified an inability to increase the capacity of a group of local Hospital Trusts, then this offered central government the opportunity to avoid the capital cost of an expansion of hospital buildings on these sites. All ISTC building projects would be underwritten by the private sector. Furthermore no additional central funding would be needed to operate the ISTC concept because PCTs would merely take those service charges out of the Hospital Trust's purse. A classical political win-win situation.

Fixing the Income Generated by Hospital Trusts

Hospital income has for decades been agreed at a local level by advanced negotiation with the DoH's devolved budget holders. The title of the local budget holder has changed many times over the years but the principle remained much the same. An agreement at the beginning of each financial year underpinned the likely level of clinical activity so that both sides could adjust their resources accordingly. However there were big variations over the UK in the rates paid for similar types of clinical activity. For example Hospital Trusts situated in East Anglia appeared to be under-funded compared with those Hospital Trusts closer to London.

Under this sort of management strategy, the local Hospital Trust managers would try to persuade doctors to limit the scope of investigation, reduce repetitive testing, prescribe within specific guidelines, and reduce outpatient follow-up appointments. Whilst this ethos reflected an attitude towards good housekeeping the motive was to keep expenditure within a predetermined budget rather than aiming for a best patient management strategy.

Another *tranche* of political mischief-making was to allow patients to choose the hospital at which they wished to be seen and treated. This had the potential to make forward budgeting very difficult both for the Hospital Trusts and their local budget holders. The unwritten political agenda was to allow those Hospital Trusts which performed poorly to go to the wall. Unfortunately there was a very poor level of information available to the public for them to make an informed choice. Furthermore emergency patients, who made up the vast majority of admissions to hospital, had little or no choice of the hospital to which the ambulance might take them. In order to reduce the regional variations in the tariffs paid for services rendered the DoH announced in 2005 that it was formulating a more equitable bill of tariffs under the heading "Payment by Results" (PbR).

In 2006 PbR was finally introduced but the lengthy delay caused a planning blight for Hospital Trusts because without the details of these tariffs they were unable to plan ahead. This was especially cogent where capital developments had to be costed against revenue forecasts. PFI projects were particularly vulnerable because with every month delaying the signing off of a contract would increase construction costs by >0.4%. For example with a £175m construction project a delay of 12 months would increase the cost by at least £9m.

Initially the term Payment by Results appeared to infer that payment was related to clinical outcome. In fact remuneration was driven by a system that was flexed by what appeared to be specific diagnostic categories and average historical length of inpatient stay. In reality the diagnosis for medical emergencies is often vague and a best guess of the cause for the patient's current problem. The intention was for the system to act as a surrogate marker for the complexity of each completed clinical episode. In the private sector each item of service would have been added to the patient's bill rather than adding a factor to augment the perceived cost of the patient's management profile.

At first sight this might appear to be a more equitable way of remunerating Hospital Trusts for the actual work carried out. Sadly, this golden opportunity to address the inadequate service to hospital patients was compromised by a financial cap imposed by the PCTs on all activities which lowered the average waiting times below the DoH's targets. It was as if over-performance was as financially punitive for the Hospital Trusts as under-performance. A better than average service to patients would carry penalties. Inevitably this sort of budgeting arrangement could lead to management looking for the ways to maximise their income rather than the service profile being driven by patient need or best clinical practice.

An example of how this approach could affect income is given below.

Case History

A 60 year old man with a 10 year history of Chronic Obstructive Pulmonary Disease (COPD) had experienced an increase in breathlessness over a few days. He lived alone in his own house and worked as a clerical officer at a supermarket. He had spent most of the last 24 hours sitting in an armchair. At about 04.00 he became aware of a pain the left side of his chest. The pain gradually worsened and at 06.00 he called his doctors' surgery. The call was diverted to an emergency answering service (Call Centre) and after a laboured conversation he was advised to call for an ambulance. The ambulance arrived within 10 minutes and took him to the nearest A&E Department.

On arrival (06.40) he was assessed by the triage nurse and examined by the junior doctor on call. Some bilateral ankle oedema was found. He had a Peak Flow (PEFR) of 200l/min.

Haematology profile (FBC), Blood chemistry, D-Dimer & Arterial blood gasses (ABG) were requested.

An ECG was recorded and a request for a chest X-ray (CXR) was made.

He was given some Co-codamol for the chest pain and some nebulised Salbutamol. PEFR increased to 300l/min.

At 10.30 he was reviewed.

His breathing was slightly less laboured. The left sided chest pain was slightly less troublesome. ECG showed inferior myocardial ischaemia. CXR showed hyper-inflated lung fields and prominent broncho-vascular shadowing and an area of translucency on the left side which could be an emphysematous bulla or a small pneumothorax.

FBC and blood chemistry were unremarkable. D-Dimer +ve.

At 10.39 he was transferred to the Emergency Assessment Unit (EAU), because if he had stayed in A&E any longer he would have breached the 4 hour waiting time target.

At 11.00 he was seen by a new group of doctors in the EAU.

They decided that he should have a Doppler U/S of both legs to exclude a Deep Venous Thrombosis (DVT) and at 16.00 the ECG should be repeated and blood should be taken for Cardiac Troponin in order to exclude myocardial damage i.e. the Acute Coronary Syndrome (ACS) or a Myocardial Infarct (MI).

Treatment with oral steroids and Clarithromycin were started (PH of penicillin allergy) on the assumption that the exacerbation of breathlessness had been caused by a chest infection.

At 14.00 he was seen by the duty Consultant Physician.

The Doppler U/S had excluded a DVT and therefore pulmonary embolic disease was less likely. The translucency on the left side of the CXR was thought to be a small left sided pneumothorax and a radiological opinion was requested.

At 18.00 the Troponin test result was reported as "undetected". ACS and MI had been excluded.

PLAN: Repeat CXR in morning.
    If CXR unchanged, PEFR improving & chest pain less, then discharge home.

The first scenario assumes that the patient is discharged on the following day with a diagnosis of:

"Chest Infection causing an exacerbation of COPD".

The second scenario takes over on the following day if the above conditions were not met and might be as follows:

Day 2. On review PEFR marginally better and CXR unchanged but chest pain still causing some concern.

PLAN: Transfer to Respiratory Ward.
11.00 Seen by Respiratory Team. ABG now showing mild hypoxia.
CT pulmonary angiography (CTPA) study ordered to exclude pulmonary embolism. Loading dose of heparin given.
15.00 CTPA performed – result negative. Translucency on left side confirmed to be an emphysematous bulla. Heparin therapy discontinued.
Treadmill Test (ETT) requested to assess coronary artery status.
Day 3. ETT had to be terminated prematurely because of breathlessness. Cardiology Team asked to see patient with a view to performing coronary angiography (CA).
Day 5. General condition improved. PEFR 350l/m. ABG within normal limits.
CA performed. Non critical coronary artery narrowing found.
Day 6. Discharged home on usual medication

The second scenario involved a longer stay in hospital, assessment by two additional medical teams and some complicated investigations, but the final diagnosis on discharge remained:

"Chest Infection causing an exacerbation of COPD".

In theory the patient could have been discharged home from the A&E Department within 4 hours because the clinical outcome was not influenced by the subsequent stay in hospital or the investigations performed. In a bed crisis, with a patient who could be satisfactorily reassured that he would be safe at home, and a GP who would take over his subsequent management this might have been a reasonable alternative strategy.

The Hospital Trust would have earned £70 for its efforts but spent more than that on investigating the clinical problem.

The patient would have had to have paid £6.85 for the antibiotic prescribed.

The patient could also have been discharged on day 2 of his hospital stay provided that there was adequate patient reassurance and GP backup.

The Hospital Trust would have earned £412 for its efforts but spent more than that on investigating the clinical problem.

If the patient had been discharged at any stage after day 2 even if the patient had stayed for 14 days

The Hospital Trust would still only have earned £2,250 for its efforts.

Clearly, keeping the patient in hospital for 3 days instead of 1 day is the most profitable outcome for the Hospital Trust but not necessarily the best clinical management plan. Furthermore it would have been clinically legitimate to ascribe the oedema of the legs to cardiac failure and in that case:

The Hospital Trust would have earned £2,360 for its efforts.

Following discharge from hospital on day 3 it would have been reasonable for an ETT and the subsequent CA to have been performed as an outpatient.

The Hospital Trust could have earned an additional £1,205

After being discharged, following the initial admission, the CA could have been performed as a later inpatient episode with a hospital stay of 3 days then:

The Hospital Trust would have earned an additional £2,918

LENGTH	INVESTIGATIONS	REMUNERATION (£)		UNDERFUNDED
OF		NHS	PRIVATE	NHS ACTIVITY
STAY			Hotel* + Tests	(£)
< 4 hours	A, B, D, E, F, G	70	NA + 225	> 155
> 4 hours day 1	H, F, C,	412	150 + 388	> 126
Day 2	G, E, J	412	300 + 672	> 560
Day 3	I	2,250	450 + 767	OK
Day 4		2,250	600 + 767	OK
Day 5	K	2,250	750 + 1,877	> 377
Day 6	E	2,250	900 + 1,972	> 622
10 days		2,250	1,500 + 1,972	> 1,222

A = FBC(£10.13), B = Chemistry(£7.46), C = Troponin(£21.67), D = D-Dimer(£29.10), E = ABG(£97.46) *lab off site*, F = ECG(£26), G = CXR(£55), H = Leg Doppler u/s(£115), I = ETT(£95), J = CTPA(£200), K = CA(£1,110),

*Private "hotel" charges make no allowance for medication or medical fees. In the private sector profits come from the prudent management of accommodation, catering and non-medical staffing.

The Hospital Trust's daily bed charges have to include all medication and a proportion of the expenditure on human resources necessary to support such a complex service plus investigations and clinical procedures.

(The current nursing establishment for a 30 bedded acute NHS medical ward would contribute £78 to each bed day. This is considerably more than the contribution of nursing support to any private facility.)

In whatever way one devises the financial arrangement:

1. Those in control of the funding mechanism will not want to give the medical professionals a licence to print money by allowing them freedom to extend management boundaries or invoke non essential investigations or procedures.
2. The medical professionals will not want the managers to impose limits on their investigational and management freedom because this could adversely affect the patient's clinical outcome.

This example underlines the difficulties inherent in fixing a funding tariff applicable to the management of medical emergencies because of the very wide scope for individual patient variation. Creating an artificial tariff derived from average NHS expenditure on similar emergencies throughout the UK merely offers Hospital Trusts the opportunity to manipulate the recovery of expenditure rather than focussing on best clinical practice.

The costs relating to planned surgical procedures are relatively easy to quantify and subject to minimal variation particularly if the patient is clinically fit. There can be no great surprise why this is the only scenario which the private sector wants to cash in on.

The number of emergencies treated in any period of time and the complexity of each patient's management are almost unquantifiable. It might be better for the emergency budget to be geared to actual expenditure so that there is no opportunity either for the Hospital Trust to massage the service profile to maximise their income or for the PCT to under resource the management of emergencies.

The North East Essex Experience

This is an example of how hospital services in North East Essex have been chronically blighted by a series of disjointed political agendas and a lack of focus on clinically important interactions between patients and healthcare providers.

In 1970 there was a concerted effort to centralise all hospital services on a new site three miles distant from the centre of town where the main hospital had been standing since 1819. The plan received initial approval. It meant that the town and its environs would be provided with a properly resourced Casualty Department and modernised inpatient accommodation. The six hospitals, which had previously contributed to that service, but were dispersed over a 20 mile radius, could then be closed. In 1973 the DoH withdrew their support, insisting that a smaller modular "*nucleus*" hospital should be built first with the transfer of some of the existing medical and surgical services and that this would be followed, after an unspecified lapse of time, by the transfer of the other services into similarly constructed modules attached appropriately to the "*nucleus*". Thirteen years later the "*nucleus*" hospital was opened but none of the six hospitals where medical and surgical patients had previously been treated could be closed because other specialties still had patients on those sites. The main blood transfusion service was now situated in the "*nucleus*" hospital three miles, and across the other side of a busy town, from the maternity hospital. The paediatric service was split between the "*nucleus*" hospital and their special care baby unit (SCBU) in the maternity hospital. The rationalisation for medical patients left the bed numbers largely unchanged although 90 medical beds were now available in the "*nucleus*" hospital. This concentrated inpatient services on five sites instead of six. Over the next six years medical services were withdrawn from three of these sites because the viability of medical training for junior doctors working on those sites had become untenable. (A probable risk overlooked by the bean counters in 1973 and again 12 years later.) These medical bed closures coincided with the transfer of Orthopaedics, Obstetrics and Gynaecology to a new stand alone building on the "*nucleus*" site, but not as an integrated module as planned in 1985. However, in this exercise 50 medical beds were lost without any reduction in the size of the population served. Furthermore the "*nucleus*" hospital could not accommodate more medical beds without reshuffling the pack. This resulted in Chest Medicine finding themselves "sharing" an Orthopaedic ward. By now <u>Medical and Elderly (COTE) emergencies</u> could no longer be accommodated within the "*nucleus*" and therefore a demountable prefabricated building was erected near the "*nucleus*" to cope with this shortfall. In 1998 another new stand alone building was erected on the "*nucleus*" site to accommodate all the remaining COTE inpatients. Once again this building was quite separate and, just to add to the difficulties in moving patients and staff around the site, it was built half a story higher than the "*nucleus*" instead of excavating the foundations to the same level. This money saving ploy (£100,000) put in jeopardy the survival of inpatients in that building when an emergency arose at night because of the tortuous route which had to be negotiated by junior medical staff on call.

In 2000 a serious attempt was made to rationalise the services on this site and transfer Oncology, ENT, Ophthalmology and Dermatology which had been left behind at the town's historic hospital building. Furthermore Biochemistry and Microbiology were still on two different sites distant from the "*nucleus*" hospital and needed urgent integration. The whole scheme was estimated to cost about £145m. By now the health ministry's new PFI scheme was in operation and was considered to be the most appropriate mechanism for funding such an expensive and complicated building programme. An application was made to the DoH. The application was approved and supported by an enabling grant of £2.4m.from the Treasury.

By the beginning of 2006 the cost of the scheme had escalated to £180m and the unitary charge, (the annual payment to the private consortia for the construction and subsequent facilities management for the next 30 years), had risen to £23m per annum which represented 13% of projected annual income. Savings derived from the closure of redundant sites and the cost efficiencies afforded by operating from a single well connected site amounted to £9m, leaving a potential annual deficit of £14m. Moreover, the certainty of an assured income trail was in limbo because the tariffs for PbR had not been finalised. Clearly without any scope to ratchet up operating income such a scheme appeared to be financially unaffordable.

During the five years that the scheme was developed the Trust's project team remained largely unchanged and well focussed upon patient needs. Unfortunately, a change in the Trust Board Chief Executive, Chairman and Director of Finance occurred in 2004/2005. Additionally the perpetual reorganisation endemic in the NHS resulted in significant changes in the two layers of management between the DoH and the Trust Board. The ideal scenario for losing the plot. Furthermore the threat of building an ISTC in the county meant that affordability had to allow for an additional £8m levy (20% of planned surgery) as part of the PCT's guarantee to provide patients for any ISTC.

In June 2006 the Trust Board abandoned the project. A large undisclosed sum of tax payer's money was paid out to compensate the private consortium for services rendered in addition to £3m spent by the Trust on working up the project. The hospital managers openly congratulated themselves for having averted a potential financial disaster. The PFI consortium disappeared without trace having lost out on what might have been a very profitable venture.

The potential patient clientele for the Hospital Trust, the majority of whom would have arrived as emergencies and therefore been unable to choose the quality of the service available, were denied the dignity and privacy which they would have received had the building project gone ahead as originally planned. By 2008 the make do and mend mentality of the Hospital Trust had accumulated eleven demountable/temporary/prefabricated buildings distributed over its site and thereby compromised any future centralisation project.

A patient focussed service had been allowed to give way to political expediency. This blow might have been softened if the Trust Board had had a financially viable alternative that was able to deliver a modernised centralised service and achieve similar standards addressing patient dignity and privacy. However, although the Trust Board had a monopoly of spin they were inspirationally bankrupt and paralysed by the government's unyielding headlock on funding procedures.

Rationing Medical Resources

The threat of rationing is probably the most divisive and ethically controversial aspect of healthcare. However this is a strictly political issue because it is driven by financial constraints. In a democracy we vote for those politicians whom we think will deliver our needs at the lowest personal cost (taxation). The proportion of the national budget consumed by healthcare will depend on how much is given to Education, the Police, the Armed Forces, Transport, the Environment and other government departments. This is all about fiscal rationing. We blindly believe that the Politicians know what is best and that they will spend our taxes wisely. Sometimes it is hard to give them credibility for this. If we passionately believe that not enough is being spent on healthcare would we prefer increased taxation or a redistribution of the budget?

A theoretical solution might be to allow all tax payers to decide what proportion of their individual tax burden should be spent on healthcare, education, the environment etc. This might be a nightmare to administer but at least it would demonstrate what democracy is all about.

Once the healthcare budget has been allocated, the Healthcare Politicians decide who gets what. Essentially this is healthcare rationing. It is difficult to make decisions which are even-handed. Where there is rationing there will always be winners and losers.

Logically less should be spent on the healthcare problems of those people whose choice of lifestyle has had a detrimental effect on their health. For example patients who develop chronic obstructive pulmonary disease (COPD), ischaemic heart disease (IHD) or lung cancer as a result of active tobacco smoking might find themselves having to finance a proportion of the cost of their healthcare needs. This could descend into a medico-legal quagmire and the main beneficiaries would be the lawyers! Alternatively this proscription of free healthcare might be applied to those who continue to abuse their health after the association between their unhealthy lifestyle and their disease profile has been explained to them.

Where would disease prophylaxis feature in this potential free for all? Immunisation against infectious diseases might be seen as a laudable use of public money because it not only protects the recipient from disease associated mortality and morbidity but also reduces the burden of disease on the non-immunised community.

Should this apply to infectious diseases acquired as a result of a person's choice to expose them self to a calculated risk of infection? Sexually transmitted diseases would be a prime target for this exception.

Where should immunisation against cancer of the cervix, caused by the human papilloma virus, feature in this calculation? The currently available vaccine against cervical cancer is projected to confer a disease reduction of 70%. It is claimed that 1000 women in the UK die from the effects of cervical cancer every year. It is estimated that the cost of the vaccine, at £250 per shot, to immunise all twelve year old girls (roughly 400,000) would be £100m per annum. Does such a huge financial outlay make sound economical sense? Why is this vaccine so expensive when a flu jab (a similar inactivated viral vaccine) costs less than £10 per shot? If the government intends to purchase such large quantities of the human papilloma virus vaccine then there should be better control over the profits made by the pharmaceutical industry or at least the scope to tax those profits more effectively and return the money to the healthcare budget.

Are there alternative approaches?

The prevalence of the human papilloma virus and the incidence of cancer of the cervix are lower in ethnic communities where male circumcision is the norm. Is there a place for the conversion of the British to Islam or Judaism, or should the Pope declare that Christians should include male circumcision in their ritual dogma? These ritual procedures would cost the NHS nothing and would additionally reduce the budget for treating the remaining cases of cervical cancer.

Should rationing be imposed on specific disease profiles?

For example one might impose a limit on what should be spent on the diagnosis and treatment of prostate cancer. It has been argued that the early diagnosis of prostate cancer might reduce the eventual expenditure on treating the condition. To this end a test for Prostate Specific Antigen (PSA) in the blood of men was once hailed as a cost effective solution. What was spent on screening would be recouped by not having to spend so much on treatment. Unfortunately the PSA test is expensive. The test population is vast and false positive results generate an abortive sequence of expensive unpleasant investigations. If you apply the principle of rationing to the budget for prostate cancer then this particular testing policy would reduce the funds available for the treatment of patients with the proven definitive disease but without significantly reducing the burden of disease requiring treatment.

One could tackle this situation from the other end. Spending less money on expensive disease management strategies when less expensive equally effective strategies are available, would allow one to spend more money on early disease detection or prevention. In this respect if orchidectomy, a simple relatively inexpensive surgical procedure, was used to treat prostate cancer, instead of giving the patient regular injections of an expensive hormone (more than £1000 per annum), particularly since both treatment strategies are equally effective, then more of the budget would be available for population screening.

How would you tackle the latest health hazard – obesity? A condition which is almost wholly self-inflicted. Food is so cheap in relation to GDP that apart from dietary education in early life the solution would be both to pay the farmers a less miserly price for their produce and impose a tax at the point of purchase on the most fattening products. Alternatively food rationing could be reintroduced. There was little obesity in the UK while food rationing was still in place after World War Two.

Measures aimed at risk reduction by statistically driven medical interventions such as giving healthy subjects cholesterol lowering drugs, is an area of healthcare where the individual might have to contribute to the cost of treatment. The logic is that the medication could be seen as a personal gamble. The treatment increases the chances of winning or, as in this case, it decreases the chance of losing, but it guarantees nothing since less than 1:100 healthy subjects are likely to benefit!

The combinations and computations of these global disease management strategies are almost limitless but wholly in the jurisdiction of the politicians. It is the role of the medical profession to make decisions on the delivery of healthcare. However, the medical profession must guard against being seen to be able to manipulate its source of remuneration to its own financial advantage and at the expense of either the patient or the tax payer.

The Public/Private Medical Conflict of Interest

Is it possible to reengage the medical profession after 60 years of arbitrary political decision making? Is it possible to disconnect the medical profession from the previous financial advantages enjoyed by having their fingers in both public and private pies? Is the medical profession too engrossed with what they are doing to be bothered with political posturing? This is the legacy of the arrangements made on behalf of the profession by Lord Moran with Nye Bevan in 1948.

In theory the argument for empowering a full-time salaried healthcare service would be that it would remove the loopholes for exploiting either the sick or the source of remuneration. Legislation could not outlaw private practice but it could draw an absolute dividing line between the two. Those in private practice could have the opportunity to be hired by the public sector to fulfil temporary shortfalls in manpower, but those working in the public sector would be barred from spending their spare time feeding at the private trough. It might be argued that in the public sector the medical profession should decide issues relating to the quality of service available and central government should be obliged to foot the bill. This approach has not been supported by successive administrations preferring instead to make these decisions at ministerial level. In the private sector these issues were always decided by market forces.

With a salaried service the risk is that it would kill off the motivation of doctors to improve the service. The minimalists would not contribute their fair share to the burden of providing the service because the financial reward would be the same no matter how many patients you treated or however many hours you worked.

Perhaps one should re-examine the rationale for having a Hospital Service and how it should work to complement healthcare delivered in the community?

In most instances the main function of Hospital Trusts is the management of Medical and Surgical Emergencies. The staffing profile should therefore reflect this functional requirement. Dealing with planned surgical procedures and outpatients would then be seen as subsidiary core activities. Emergency work requires appropriately trained staff and backup from a broad spectrum of investigational facilities and Specialists including those whose main contribution to healthcare is not based on medical or surgical emergencies, e.g. Dermatologists and Rheumatologists. In the past, a doctor "on call" might also be performing an outpatient session, carrying out planned investigational procedures, working in the operating theatre or even be "off site". This multi-tasking activity compromises the care of emergencies. The prompt availability of senior staff in the emergency arena is an essential part of good practice. Therefore when a member of staff is contracted to work with emergencies for a specified period of time, it is important that that person should not be expected to perform additional duties outside the Emergency Department.

When patients are transferred from the Emergency Department to a Medical or Surgical ward, continuity of care might be facilitated if their Emergency Consultant subsequently spent some time in charge of their management in that less acute arena. In this way there could be a rotation of each person's work schedule both during their immediate postgraduate training and later as a Consultant.

For example the Junior Doctor, whose overall experience would be gained by exposure to a sequence of many different medical or surgical specialties, could spend two months out of every six months in the Emergency Department. This could then be followed by four months working in the less acute activities of caring for inpatients and attending the outpatient department. Likewise a pair of Consultants could spend a week in the Emergency Department, followed by two weeks supervising the care of their specialty's inpatients, and then devote the remaining five weeks of this eight week cycle to servicing their specialty's outpatient commitment. Such a sequential work pattern would alleviate the stress generated when working solely with emergencies.

This sort of pre-planned mono-tasking work pattern would be difficult to implement if Consultants continued to go off to service their private practice, where they might be expected to see their privileged patients at short notice and consequently find themselves temporarily having to abandon their commitment to the public sector. A compromise might be to allow any private medical activity only when the incumbent was scheduled for outpatient duties. In that case Emergency Department and inpatient rotas would be sacrosanct and not amenable to negotiation.

Dealing with outpatient referrals and planned surgical activities would require an agreed service provision by each specialty which laid down the minimum number of patients seen or procedures carried out per session per Consultant. This level of activity would be geared to achieving a predetermined waiting time. Where demand exceeded the existing human resources then more Consultant posts would have to be established. During short term shortfalls of activity or where target waiting times are reduced by political dictat then the temporary secondment of Consultants from the private sector could be employed to clear the backlog. However, the additional funding required to achieve such targets would have to come directly from the Treasury and not out of previously earmarked local healthcare funds.

The work pattern of Consultants in the private sector tends to be multifunctional with different aspects of patient care taken on by Consultant colleagues. In the public sector there has been an historical leaning towards a hierarchical method of working with the Consultant being the last person to see the patient. This has certain educational advantages if specific junior doctors and the Consultant form part of the same team. The mechanism worked well in the UK when hours of work were flexed around the functionality of the team. With the application of the European Working Time Directive to healthcare staff, specialty team functionality became fragmented, particularly in District General Hospitals where the human resources of each team were limited. Furthermore continuity of patient care was compromised with a tendency for patient management to become a game of pass the patient. This is in stark contrast to patient management in the private sector where patient and Consultant tend to become joined at the hip, in part for fear of losing control of the money trail. Additionally the hierarchical division of labour compromises patient safety in the Emergency Department where patients are better served by a *hands on* approach by all members of the team in order to avoid delays in initiating the most appropriate investigations and treatment.

Another divisive impediment to patient management in the hospital setting is the arbitrary definition of patients over a certain age as *"elderly or geriatric"* and consequently in need of the attention of a separate group of Specialists. All junior doctors spend time learning about the ways in which disease may be modified by the ageing process and General Practitioners see all patients irrespective of age. Why therefore is it necessary to redefine older medical patients in hospital as *"elderly"*? This probably reflects an attitude which evolved several decades ago when the elderly hospital patient with poor social circumstances and medical problems of a chronic and disabling nature were perceived to be "bed blockers". What they actually required was not a new breed of Hospital Consultants – the Geriatricians – but a revamped properly funded social services facility. Consequently fully trained junior hospital doctors wishing to remain in the hospital service but lacking the opportunities to join a specialty group opted to join the ranks of the Geriatricians. This usually meant that a Junior Doctor could become a Consultant in Geriatric Medicine at an earlier age than they would have done had they waited for an appropriate opening in their previously chosen medical specialty.

The latest addition to the list of medical specialties is the Consultant in Emergency Medicine. The plan was that this breed of Consultant would be similar to an A&E Consultant except that they would deal exclusively with Medical Emergencies leaving Trauma and surgical problems under the care of the A&E Consultant. Their role would be as a *hands on* group of Consultants working exclusively in the Emergency Department alongside the junior doctors in a non-hierarchical team. This would be good for patients during the acute phase of their illness but continuity of care thereafter might be fragmented. Large long-established teaching hospitals would be the main beneficiaries. Smaller District General Hospitals might struggle to cover the department 24/7 without at least 4 Consultants in post. With 24/7 cover in the Emergency Department those Consultants, from the other medical specialties, who had previously flitted in and out of the Emergency Department, might find their "on call" role removed from their contracts and their salary docked accordingly. A lack of exposure to the acute phase of medical emergencies would be likely to lead to their becoming deskilled and less able to handle medical emergencies arising in their inpatient clientele. The risk for the Emergency Consultant might be an inability to sustain their enthusiasm throughout a 30 year contract. A change of specialty at a later date would require retraining and might involve a temporary reduction in salary. There might also be a reluctance of the established specialty Consultants to accept an ageing colleague into their ranks. There is no parallel Emergency Specialty in the private sector and therefore no opportunity to enhance income by dipping into the private cookie jar.

The risk to the new Emergency Specialty is that it might attract the "no hopers" looking for speedy promotion in an under-populated Specialty.

Is it not curious that we employ Junior Doctors for 8 – 12 years in the acute medical arena where they gain considerable experience and expertise only to suggest that on attaining Consultant status they should no longer be exposed to acute medical decision making and adopt a somewhat sedentary role instead?

The need for senior doctors at the coalface in the Emergency Department is not in question. We need to establish the best way of addressing the problem and not necessarily accept that the plans of the Medical Colleges offer the best solution for both patients and the workforce. The innovative use of existing medical staff, with appropriate enhancement of human resources in order to re-establish team structures previously eroded by politically motivated working time directives, is another approach.

Changing the emphasis of healthcare provision within the public sector might help to reinvigorate medical research and rekindle an interest in the academic approach to knowledge gathering as opposed to the testing of the disease management strategies of the pharmaceutical industry.

The challenge to the medical profession is very clear. This is not a game of political football. Openness is paramount. The rewards could be earth shattering. Achieving this goal is well within the intellectual abilities of such a highly qualified group of professionals.

Conclusion

Maintaining the health of the population does not have to be fought out on a battleground between those who provide the resources and those who deliver the service. Funding mechanisms for healthcare in the UK need to be changed. Hospital Trusts can not be expected to pay for major developments from service generated income. Either the Treasury needs to pay for capital projects up front or local industry needs to be empowered to support their local Hospital Trust by favourable tax avoidance schemes which raise their profile as community sensitive beneficiaries without compromising their profitability. This approach might be preferable to the current practice whereby some companies provide their employees with limited private healthcare insurance.

The budget for healthcare delivered outside Hospital has to be clearly separated from that delivered by the Hospital Trusts. The artificial creation of competitive bargaining between these different facets of healthcare delivery introduce unnecessary patient insensitive obstacles.

The medical profession needs to reinvent its approach to the delivery of healthcare. This will require soul-searching and a determination to work together without being caught up in personal empire building. Those whose wallets weigh more heavily on their hearts than their souls need to be separated from those who have a more compassionate approach to the sick, but without the latter being seen as inferior beings or financially compromised. However those who choose to devote their energies to the public sector need to have a robust work ethic with pre-determined "productivity" activities geared to achieving waiting time initiatives.

Management needs to accept that priority should be given to the quality of the service and must be seen to be respecting patient dignity and privacy. Management is there to facilitate the delivery of the service and not to dictate its clinical functionality. Where politically driven targets are espoused the emphasis should be on enhancing the human resources available in the public sector or by temporarily inviting those in the private sector to operate within the public sector at a rate commensurate with that applicable within the public domain.

Rationing the scope of the service is likely to remain a reality. The introduction of new technology and novel treatments will have to be funded by central government. This is where politicians can earn their brownie points and not by the imposition of empirical targets.

The future of healthcare for our people will depend upon the commitment of the politicians and the healthcare professionals to deliver a service without fear or favour and free at the point of delivery. Unless there is mutual ownership of the service by all contributors, divisiveness will continue to handicap the delivery of best practice.

In: Global Privatization and Its Impact
Editors: I.J. Hagen and T.S. Halvorsen, pp. 27-45

ISBN: 978-1-60456-785-4
© 2008 Nova Science Publishers, Inc.

Chapter 2

PRIVATIZATION, COMPETITION AND PERFORMANCE: EVIDENCE FROM AUSTRALIA

Isaac Otchere[*]

Sprott School of Business, Carleton University,
1125 Colonel By Drive, Ottawa, ON, K1S 5B6, Canada

Abstract

We take stock of the performance of share issue privatizations in Australia and find that consistent with our conjecture that investors expected the privatization to significantly impact on industry counterparts through industrial repositioning, the industry counterparts reacted negatively to the privatization announcements. In the long term, the privatized firms outperformed the market index and the industry counterparts. We also find that the firms privatized by the Federal (Commonwealth) Government had significant market impact than those privatized by State Governments. In terms of operating performance, we observe that the privatized firms have become more profitable in the post privatization period than in the pre privatization period, but their operating efficiency has not significantly improved. The privatization has also led to a significant attrition in staff levels, especially in the years immediately following the year of privatization. Our results show that after controlling for contemporaneous economy-wide factors, share issue privatization has yielded significant stock market and operating performance improvements for privatized firms in Australia.

Keywords: Privatization; industry competitors' reaction; abnormal returns, operating performance.

JEL Classification: G21, G32, G 14

---

[*] E-mail address: iotchere@sprott.carleton.ca. Tel: (613) 520-2600 ext 2731. Fax: (613) 520-4427

1. Introduction

Privatization has become a notable feature of restructuring state-owned enterprises. The potential for improvement in performance of state-owned enterprises, and the need to raise revenue for the state are some of the reasons for the popularity of privatization programs. Governments of all persuasions in both developed and developing countries have privatized and continue to privatize state-owned enterprises. In Australia, both the Federal (Commonwealth) and State Governments of different political leanings have privatized publicly-owned enterprises. Australia has had one of the largest privatization programs among OECD countries; its value of privatizations ranks second after the UK in terms of the value of privatization, and second after New Zealand in terms of relative size of GDP (Reserve Bank of Australia (1997)). While better operating performance of privatized firms has been documented for a number of countries, this is yet to be confirmed for Australia.

Privatizations in Australia have typically taken two forms, namely trade sales and public floats. For many state-owned enterprises, privatization was undertaken after the firms had passed through a corporatization phase. The purpose of corporatization was to allow the government-owned firms to operate on commercial basis before being privatized.[1] This allowed the firms' financial position to be strengthened before privatization so that they can be sold for a higher price. State owned enterprises have been sold at both the State and Commonwealth levels of Government in Australia. In the 1990s, the Australian Governments garnered over $70 billion from the sale of business and assets owned by the state (Share, April 2000). According to the Reserve Bank of Australia (1997), the largest proceeds were realized from the privatization of Electricity (VIC) which generated AUD$22.5 billion from the asset sale, followed by Telstra and Commonwealth Bank, with these firms realizing $14.3 billion and $8.1 billion respectively.[2] Almost 15 years have passed since the government initiated the privatization program but there has not been any systematic analysis of the performance of privatized firms. Since one of the reasons for privatization is to improve the performance of the privatized firms, it is appropriate to take stock of the performance of the privatized firms in an OECD country that has had a significant number of privatizations. This study examines the operating and financial performance of the firms privatized through share issue privatization.

Extant literature has documented mixed results in terms of the post privatization performance of the former state-owned enterprises. Whereas Megginson et al (1994), Boubakri and Cosset (1998) and Otchere and Chan (2003) among others document significant improvement in performance of privatized firms; others including Aggarwal et al (1993) and Omran (2002) find significant underperformance of privatized firms. Prior studies have also shown that the outcomes of privatization tend to vary with a country's level of development (Dewenter and Malatesta, 2001). A related strand of literature has shown that a country's level of governance and institutional development can affect the performance of privatized firms (e.g., Ramamurti, 2000; Dyck, 2001; Shirley, 2001). This feature constitutes a major difference between privatization outcomes in developed and developing countries, since the

---

[1] Under corporatization, the state-owned enterprises were maintained under public ownership, but were required to achieve certain commercial benchmarks, pay tax, borrow funds without government guarantee and have any regulatory advantages removed.

[2] Australian privatization has been discussed in detail in Lee et al (2002)

governance mechanisms are relatively weak in the latter. While superior operating performance (efficiency) has been confirmed in a number of studies especially in industrialized countries, this is the first time the effects of privatization have been systematically examined for Australia (a country whose privatization program ranks second among OECD countries in terms of GDP). We add to the privatization studies by examining the privatization program of one of the first OECD countries to embark on an elaborate privatization program. Country-specific studies such as the current one have the advantage of avoiding problems relating to differences in institutional environment, as issue that plagues cross country studies.

Also, the majority of the privatization research has been concerned with the effects of privatization on the performance of the privatized firms. However, privatization has implications that are likely to affect the performance of other firms in the industry. In so far as ownership and competition are important aspects of privatization, the privatization of state owned enterprises will impact on the performance of rivals through industrial repositioning of firms to capture and retain market share. This implication, however, has been overlooked by most prior researchers. The exception is Eckel et al (1997) and Otchere and Chan (2005) who respectively analyze the effects of the privatization of the British Airways and the Commonwealth Bank of Australia on their rivals. We submit that the aggressive actions taken by the new owners or managers of the privatized firms can affect product prices and competition in the industry. Hence, using a sample of Australian firms which were privatized between 1992 and 1998 (there has not been any significant privatization since then) this study examines the effect of privatization on industry counterparts.

We find that the industry counterparts reacted negatively to the privatization announcements. Also, contrary to the evidence documented for private sector initial public offerings, our sample of public sector initial share issue privatizations outperforms the market index and their industry counterparts over the first three post-listing years. Firms privatized by the Federal (Commonwealth) Government had significant market effects than those announced by State Governments. In terms of pre and post privatization operating performance, we find that the privatized firms have become more profitable in the post privatization period than in the pre privatization period, but their operating efficiency has not significantly improved. The improvement in profitability ratios thus appears to have come from increase in revenue. On a relative basis we observe that the privatized firms have become more profitable than their industry counterparts. However, they have been less efficient than their rivals in reducing expenses. Privatization, and the attendant change in the objective of the firm to profit maximization, has also led to a significant attrition in staff levels, especially in the years immediately following the year of privatization. We note that after controlling for contemporaneous economy-wide factors, share issue privatization in Australia has yielded significant stock market and operating performance improvements. The results of this study would be of interest to investors, policy makers, regulators and governments that have embarked upon or are contemplating privatization. The rest of the paper is structured as follows: Section 2 reviews the literature on privatization, while Section 3 describes the data and sample collection procedure and outlines the methodology. Section 4 presents the results, while Section 5 concludes the study.

2. Background and Hypotheses Development

Extant literature identifies two types of problems associated with government ownership, namely, political and managerial incentive problems. Focusing on the managerial incentive problem, Vickers and Yarrow (1989) argue that the lack of monitoring of state-owned enterprises results in low-powered incentives on the part of managers to improve performance. Shleifer and Vishny (1994) suggest that political interference from governments distorts the objectives of state enterprises. Governments in most countries use state-owned enterprises (SOEs) to pursue multiple and often conflicting goals such as welfare maximization at the expense of profit maximization. For example, SOEs are used as vehicles for employment purposes. Consistent with this assertion, Boycko et al (1996) show that state-owned enterprises are significantly over-staffed. The implication of these theoretical arguments is that once governments privatize state-owned enterprises, the performance of the firm will improve, as the firms tend to reduce employment levels in the post privatization period because of the abandonment of social goals and the pursuit of profit maximization objective. One mechanism through which privatized firms enhance their competitiveness is to reduce their marginal cost by shedding labor in the post privatization period.

The question of whether privatization actually leads to improvements in efficiency and profitability has been the subject of a number of empirical studies (see Megginson and Netter, 1998 for a review of the literature). In generally, researchers have shown that privatization and the attendant change in ownership structure and the firm's objectives, together with the change in the managers' incentives often lead to a more focused and efficient organization (Megginson et al. (1994) and D'Souza et al. (2000)). The public trading of the firm's shares also facilitates the adoption of market oriented compensation plans, as management compensation can be tied to the firm's stock price. The pressures from product market competition also compel the newly privatized firms to operate more efficiently, aggressively and competitively if they are to survive in the post-privatization period. We therefore hypothesize that the performance of the privatized firms will be better after privatization.

Under government ownership, most privatized firms had market power but they had to endure pressures from the government in relation to their pricing and investment decisions. Following privatization however, most privatized firms usually retain significant market power and consequently may continue to operate as defacto monopolies while being relieved of the requirements to follow government directives designed to promote social goals. Privatized firms may be able to exploit this market power to their advantage. They can become a stronger competitive force for rivals in the industry because of their dominant position in the product market (Otchere 2005). Thus, the privatized firms, with their significant market power, could realize greater post privatization gains at the expense of their rivals. The privatization of a state enterprise could thus hurt rivals through increased competition. Based on the foregoing, we hypothesize that industry counterparts will react negatively to the privatization announcements:[3]

---

[3] Privatization announcements could also generate positive information effects for the rival firms in several ways. First, privatization could lead to the relaxation of the rules of operations in the industry which can benefit the rivals. Second, privatization usually results in the loss of non-competitive incentives such as subsidies and tax cuts that the former SOE used to enjoy. The loss of these benefits could hurt the competitive position of the newly privatized firm. Also, the fact that all firms may now be operating on a fair playing field will make the industry counterparts relatively more competitive than before.

3. Data and Methodology

The list of privatized firms was obtained from the Reserve Bank of Australia and the announcement dates were identified from Reuter's business news archives.[4] All publicly traded firms that also went public in the same year as the privatized firm were initially considered as candidates for the control group of industry counterparts. Following Barber and Lyon (1997), we included in the control group rivals that had market capitalization in the range of 80% to 120% of that of the privatized firm one month after the privatization. The pre-listing period financial statements for the newly listed firms were obtained from the firms' prospectuses. The post-listing financial statement data and stock price data for all the firms and the All Ordinary Index were obtained from Datastream. To be included in the study, we require that the privatization announcement date and stock price and financial statement data be available in the aforementioned sources. To reduce confounding effects we excluded rival firms that announced significant events such as mergers and acquisitions or earnings announcement around the event period.

Table 1. Distribution of the sample of Australian share issue privatization for the period 1990–2000*

Company	Fiscal Year of Privatization	Proceeds ($million)
Commonwealth Government Issues		
Commonwealth Serum Laboratories	1993/94	299
Commonwealth Bank of Australia	1991/92	1311
Commonwealth Bank of Australia	1993/94	1686
Commonwealth Bank of Australia	1996/97	3390
Qantas	1995/96	1450
Telstra	1997/98	14,330
Telstra	1999/00	16,500
State Government Issues		
GIO	1992/93	1260
United Energy	1995/96	1553
Tabcorp	1994/95	609
Suncorp-Metway	1997/98	610
SGIO	1993/94	165
NSW TAB	1999/00	967.5
Total	44,130.5	
Mean	6304.36	
Median	1311	

* There has not been any privatization since then.

---

[4] The announcement date relates to the first time that the government announced its intention to privatize the firm.

Descriptive statistics and frequency distribution of the sample is presented in Table 1. The mean (median) gross proceeds from the privatizations were A$6,304 million (A$ 1,131 million). The privatization of Telstra generated the largest proceeds, with the two tranches generating far more revenue for the government than all the other privatizations combined. The privatization of the SGIO generated the smallest proceeds. Of the total number of firms that were privatized during the period, 40% were sold by the Federal (Commonwealth) Government and these generated 88.28% of the total proceeds realized from privatization. By virtue of their sizes, all the firms that were sold in tranches were owned by the Federal (Commonwealth) government whereas those enterprises that were sold by the State governments were privatized in single tranches.

3.1. Methodology

Three different set of analyses are carried out in this study. First, we examine the privatization announcement effects on the industry counterparts using the market-adjusted method. To obtain market-adjusted daily abnormal returns, we adjusted the individual firm's daily returns for contemporaneous market return. Designating the announcement date as day 0, we estimated the abnormal returns over the 11 days surrounding the announcement date. The daily market-adjusted abnormal returns were then averaged across all firms. Cumulative abnormal returns were estimated by summing the daily market-adjusted returns across different event windows. Then t-tests were conducted by dividing the abnormal returns by their contemporaneous cross sectional standard errors. Second, the long run stock market performance of the sample firms was also examined by analyzing the returns of the privatized firms and those of the industry counterparts. Since the privatized firms did not have stock market data prior to the initial privatization date, we used the market-adjusted method to compute abnormal returns. We hypothesize that privatization would give the management of the privatized firms the liberty to pursue growth-oriented policies that will enable the firms to generate higher returns for investors. To examine this conjecture, we compare the 3-year post privatization returns of our privatized firms sample with the returns of the AOI (benchmark index) and those of a control sample.

Third, to ascertain whether the operating performance of the privatized firms improved after the change of ownership, we examine the pre- and post-privatization operating performance of the privatized firms using profitability, operating efficiency, leverage, investment and labor related ratios. We measure profitability by the return on sales (net income to sales), return on assets (net income to total assets) and return on equity (net income to equity) ratios. Operating efficiency is measured using cost-to-income ratio, while asset efficiency is examined using asset turnover ratio (ATO). We estimate leverage as the debt to asset ratio. Details of these measures are summarized in appendix A.

Our hypothesis is that given the change in ownership structure and the increased focus on profitability the operating performance of the privatized firms will improve after privatization. The change in operating performance is first examined by comparing the privatized firms' ratios from year -3 to year $+3$ relative to the year of privatization. Analyzing the trend in performance over the pre- and post- privatization periods is perhaps not adequate because it could be difficult to draw strong conclusions from the result (especially from the mean ratios) since these data are not adjusted for economy-wide or industry-wide factors that may affect the ratios. As Cornett and Tehranian (1992) argue, trends in the industry would affect the sample firms' performance. Thus, any significant change documented for the privatized firm could be due to factors other than privatization. Therefore, to account for the impact of possible contemporaneous events, we also report industry-adjusted median (mean) performance measures for the privatized firms. We calculated industry-adjusted performance as the difference between the privatized firms' ratios and the industry counterparts' ratios. The significance of the industry-adjusted performance measures for each year from year –3 to year +3 is tested using the Wilcoxon signed-rank test. The significance of the change in the mean pre-privatization period (year -3 to year –1) and the mean post-privatization period (year 1 to year 3) operating performance is examined with the help of a t-test.

4. Results and Analysis

4.1. Short Run Stock Market Effects

The market reaction of the industry competitors to the privatization announcement is presented in Table 2. We observe that all the abnormal returns in the event days surrounding the announcement date are negative. On the announcement date, the industry counterparts' shareholders lost 0.45% of their wealth (the returns are significant at 5%). Also, in the 3 days (5-days) surrounding the announcement date, the industry counterparts realized a significant abnormal returns of -1.07% (-0.93%). The negative market effects seem to be concentrated in the week surrounding the privatization announcement, as the abnormal returns beyond five days surrounding the announcement date are not significant at conventional levels.

Table 2. Abnormal returns realized by industry counterparts in response to privatization announcements

This table presents the abnormal returns of rival firms in response to privatization announcements in Australia over the sample period 1990-2000. Panel A shows the abnormal returns while Panel B presents the distribution of the announcement day (AR0) abnormal returns. Abnormal returns are calculated as the difference between actual returns and expected returns, with expected returns generated from the market model parameters estimated with 200 daily returns ending t-20 relative to the announcement period. Scholes and Williams adjusted beta is employed in estimating the expected returns. The symbols ***,**,* represent significance at the 1, 5, and 10 percent levels respectively.

Panel A. Cumulative (daily) abnormal returns to rival firms for different event periods

Event days	% Return	t-statistic
[-5, 5]	-0.22	0.32
[-2, 2]	-0.93	1.72*
[-1, 1]	-1.07	2.40**
[-1, 0]	-0.76	2.25**
[0]	-0.45	2.09**
[0, 2]	-0.75	1.74*
[0, 5]	-0.70	1.50

Table 2. Continued

Panel B. Distribution of rival firms' announcement date abnormal returns associated with privatization announcements

Range for Day 0 returns	Number of Day 0 abnormal returns
$2\% < AR_0$ $0\% < AR_0 < 1\%$	7
$1\% < AR_0 < 2\%$	10
$0\% < AR_0 < 1\%$	42
$-1\% < AR_0 < 0\%$	39
$-2\% < AR_0 < -1\%$	16
$AR_0 < -2\%$	13
Total	127

The market effects observed for our sample is consistent with that documented in Otchere and Chan (2003) who show that Australian banks reacted negatively to the privatization of the Commonwealth Bank of Australia. That, the industry counterparts reacted negatively to the privatization announcement is consistent with the conjecture that investors expected the privatization and the attendant rejuvenation of the former state-owned enterprises to affect the competitive position of the industry counterparts. Since these national icons are usually large and sometimes had monopoly status prior to the privatization, their sheer size gives them a competitive edge over rivals. The negative market effect documented for the industry counterparts reflects this competitive pressure that privatization brings to the industry. In the next section, we examine whether this competitive advantage translates into better stock market performance for the privatized firms.

4.2. Long Run Performance

4.2.1. Stock Market Performance

The long run cumulative abnormal returns realized by the sample firms are presented in table 3. Panel A presents the market-adjusted returns realized by the sample firms, while Panel B shows the distribution of the 3-year cumulative abnormal returns. The results presented in Panel A have been adjusted for contemporaneous market effects. There is evidence that apart from market factors, industry factors also contribute to the returns realized by firms that operate in the industry. Therefore, using the rivals' returns to control for industry influences, we estimate the industry adjusted cumulative abnormal returns as the difference between the privatized firms' abnormal returns and the industry counterparts' returns. These industry-adjusted returns are presented in column 6 and 7 of Table 3. Some interesting observations emerge from the results. First, consistent with evidence documented in extant literature, we find significant underperformance for the private sector IPOs that also went public around the time of the privatization. The cumulative abnormal returns for the private sector IPOs were -16.55%, -24.34% and -20.56% in the first, second and third years respectively following their

IPO, albeit only the first and second year results are statistically significant. On the contrary, we document significantly positive abnormal returns for our sample of government IPOs. The cumulative abnormal returns realized by the privatized firms for the first, second and third years were 7.85%, 17.48% and 19.93% respectively of which the second and third year abnormal returns are significant at the 10% and 5% respectively.[5] The positive market-adjusted cumulative abnormal returns for the privatized firms and the negative cumulative abnormal returns for the industry counterparts generate significantly positive industry- (and risk-) adjusted cumulative abnormal returns for the privatized firms of 23.35%, 29.60% and 24.95% for the first, second and third years respectively.[6] These returns are significant at the 5% level. The median returns also give similar observations.

Table 3. Long run abnormal returns to rival firms in response to privatization announcements

This table presents the three-year abnormal returns realized by the sample firms following the privatization announcements made by Australian governments over the period 1990-2000. The returns are market-adjusted cumulative abnormal returns. The cumulative market-adjusted returns are from month 1 to month 60 relative to the share issue month (month 0). Panel A shows the abnormal returns, while Panel B presents the distribution of the three year abnormal returns. The figures in parentheses are t-statistics. The symbols [***], [**], [*] indicate significance at the 1%, 5% and 10% level respectively.

Panel A. Cumulative (monthly) abnormal returns.

Window	Privatized Firms (N=13)		Rivals (N=127)		Difference	
	Mean	Median	Mean	Median	mean	median
[1, 12]	7.85	7.20	-16.55	-15.50	24.40	22.70
	(1.41)		(-2.41)[**]		(2.76)[***]	
[1, 24]	17.48	7.74	-24.34	-21.86	41.82	29.60
	(2.08)[*]		(-1.94)[*]		(2.77)[***]	
[1, 36]	19.93	7.00	-20.56	-17.95	39.87	24.95
	(2.31)[**]		(-1.54)		(2.55)[**]	

---

[5] We do not examine underpricing of Australian government sector IPOs, a phenomenon that has extensively been analyzed by Lee et al, (2002).
[6] There is evidence that new issues are more risky so this adjustment accounts for the risk of new issues.

Table 3. Continued

Panel B. Distribution of sample firms' three-year cumulative abnormal returns following the privatization announcements

CAR window	Privatized Firms	Rival Firms
50%<CAR	3	25
40%<CAR<50%	0	2
20%<CAR<40%	1	4
10%<CAR<20%	1	7
0%<CAR<10%	5	6
-10%<CAR<0%	3	22
-20%<CAR<-10%	0	7
-40%<CAR<-20%	0	8
-50%<CAR<-40%	0	3
CAR<-50%	0	43
Total	13	127

In Panel B, we show the distribution of the three-year cumulative abnormal returns for the privatized firms and the industry counterparts. We observe that 77% of the privatized firms earned positive cumulative abnormal returns in the three years following the privatization. Also, about 39% of the sample firms earned cumulative abnormal returns of less than 10%. For the private sector IPOs however, only 35% of the sample firms realized positive abnormal returns. Most of the industry counterparts realized cumulative abnormal returns of less than -20%, with 34% of the firms losing more than half of their value three years after going public. The results presented for the privatized firms are generally consistent with those reported by Otchere and Chan (2003), Verbrugge et al (1999), Levis (1993), and Menyah and Paudyal (1996) who document positive long run abnormal returns for privatized firms.

4.2.2. Operating Performance

The operating performance measures for the privatized firms and their industry counterparts are presented in Table 4. Columns 3 to 9 show the median ratios for the privatized firms and their industry counterparts, whereas columns 10-12 present the mean pre- and post-privatization ratios. We find that the privatized firms' profitability has improved significantly in the post-privatization period. Focusing on the yearly median ratios, we observe an upward trend in all the profitability measures. For example, the ROA of the privatized firms improved from 0.86% three years before the privatization to 2.73% three years after the change. Similar improvements in profit margin, ROE, and cash flow return are observed. Also, the mean post-privatization ROA (ROE) of 3.53% (17.45%) is significantly greater than the mean pre-privatization ratio of 2.66% (13.74%) and the difference is significant at 1% (5%). The mean cash flow return and profit margin show similar improvements in the post-privatization period, albeit the post-privatization profit margin is not statistically different from the pre-privatization ratio. On a relative basis we observe that the privatized firms have become more profitable than their industry counterparts, as their post-privatization profitability ratios are statistically better than those of the industry counterparts.

Table 4. Operating performance measures for the privatized firms and their industry counterparts

This table presents the univariate test of the profitability, efficiency, investment, leverage and employment related ratios of the privatized firms and their rivals. For each performance measure, the table provides median ratios for the sample for years -3 to + 3 relative to the year of privatization. The operating performance measures examined are profit margin, return on assets (ROA), return on equity (ROE), return on cash flows, expense to income ratio (TETR), asset turnover ratio (ATO), capital expenditures to sales, growth in capital expenditure, debt to asset ratio, interest coverage ratio (IC) and change in employment. The mean ratios are based on the 3 year pre- and post privatization ratios. The difference in the yearly (median) ratios is tested using the Wilcoxon Z-statistic whilst the difference in pre- and post-privatization ratios is based on t-tests. The tests are one-tailed test and the symbols ***, **, *, represent significance at 1, 5% and 10% respectively.

Performance measure		Year -3	Year -2	Year -1	Year 0	Year 1	Year 2	Year 3	Pre-privatization mean	Post-privatization mean	Difference (post-pre)
Profitability	**Profit Margin(PM)**										
	Privatized	9.12	10.25	12.29	8.69	10.42	11.63	11.33	10.04	12.65	2.61
	Rivals	3.92	3.83	6.33	6.76	6.20	7.82	6.88	2.67	3.16	0.49
	Difference	5.20	6.42*	5.96**	1.93*	4.22***	3.81***	4.45***	7.37	9.49**	
	Return on Asset (ROA)										
	Privatized	0.86	1.45	1.90	2.01	3.58	3.87	2.73	2.66	3.53	0.88*
	Rivals	1.20	1.22	0.93	1.22	0.86	0.85	0.90	-0.33	-1.24	-0.91
	Difference	-0.34	0.23*	0.97**	0.79**	2.72***	3.02***	1.83***	2.99	4.77**	
	Return on Equity(ROE)										
	Privatized	12.80	16.10	10.30	9.14	13.27	14.14	14.91	13.74	17.45	3.71**
	Rivals	4.57	8.29	8.87	8.73	7.01	7.20	11.63	5.49	5.40	-0.09
	Difference	8.23	7.81*	1.43**	0.41	6.26***	6.94***	3.28***	8.24	12.04***	
	Return on Cash Flow(RCF)										
	Privatized	1.50	1.40	1.80	6.10	8.43	8.00	7.69	6.00	11.00	5.00*
	Rivals	2.49	2.31	2.12	1.96	2.25	1.76	2.12	2.49	2.71	0.22
	Difference	-0.99	-0.91*	-0.32**	4.14***	6.18***	6.24***	5.57***	3.51	8.29**	
Efficiency	**Total Expense-to-Total Revenue(TETR)**										
	Privatized	56.92	58.57	48.83	50.19	36.91	44.16	42.87	42.96	48.47	5.51
	Rivals	17.52	28.33	25.14	25.45	43.17	23.41	24.95	33.26	37.18	3.92
	Difference	39.40	30.24*	23.69**	24.74**	-6.26***	20.75***	17.92**	9.69	11.28	

Table 4. Continued

Performance measure		Year –3	Year –2	Year –1	Year 0	Year 1	Year 2	Year 3	Preprivatization mean	Post-privatization mean	Difference (post-pre)
Cont'd											
	Asset Turnover Ratio (ATO)										
	Privatized	7.39	9.13	21.21	46.77	45.10	38.39	41.43	30.03	34.28	4.25
	Rivals	45.58	36.52	38.49	40.01	35.05	41.21	39.04	45.15	45.89	0.74
	Difference	-38.19	-27.39*	-17.28**	6.76**	10.05***	-2.82***	2.39**	-15.12	-11.60	
Investment	***Capital Expenditures/Net Sales (CENS)***										
	Privatized	2.87	5.35	3.78	4.15	6.29	5.05	3.69	6.64	6.83	0.19
	Rivals	6.34	3.87	3.61	3.60	3.51	3.56	3.14	17.22	7.30	-9.92
	Difference	-3.47	1.48*	0.17**	0.55**	2.78***	1.49***	0.55**	-10.58	-0.47	
	Growth in Capex (GC)										
	Privatized	-46.17	61.00	-3.05	3.54	8.07	3.39	-8.18	-12.74	-9.96	2.78
	Rivals	17.87	9.19	14.34	14.13	9.95	10.81	13.19	20.70	31.30	10.61
	Difference	-64.04	51.81	-17.39	-10.59*	-1.88**	-7.42**	-21.37**	-33.44	-41.26	
Leverage	***Debt to Asset Ratio (DAR)***										
	Privatized	94.45	94.21	82.78	74.30	73.02	72.94	73.86	81.12	80.43	-0.68
	Rivals	65.42	66.07	51.39	54.68	57.85	63.86	85.18	63.21	66.55	3.33
	Difference	29.03	28.14*	31.39**	19.62***	15.17***	9.08***	-11.32***	17.90	13.89	
	Interest Coverage Ratio (ICR)										
	Privatized	0.29	0.27	0.17	2.33	3.17	2.44	1.62	1.12	3.04	1.92
	Rivals	1.61	1.04	1.21	1.75	1.21	0.84	1.44	0.70	1.18	0.47
	Difference	-1.32	-0.77***	-1.04***	0.58***	1.96***	1.60***	0.18	0.41	1.86	
Employment	***Employment growth rate (ΔLabour)***										
	Privatized	-1.41	-4.14	0.73	2.35	-6.44	-1.32	0.00	-0.87	-1.74	-0.87*
	Rivals	1.14	0.00	7.63	3.45	2.03	0.61	2.26	2.20	8.42	6.22
	Difference	-2.55	-4.14	-6.90	-1.10	-8.47**	-1.93	-2.26	-3.07	-10.16***	

Turning to the efficiency ratios, we note that the privatized firms have not been able to improve their operating efficiency. First, there is no appreciable improvement in the asset turnover ratio. Second, the privatized firms mean cost-to-income ratio continues to be significantly higher than that of the industry counterparts in the post-privatization period, albeit the mean pre- and post-privatization cost-to-income ratio is not statistically different. The privatized firms' median asset turnover ratio also lags behind that of the industry counterparts. Though their debt levels have reduced in the post privatization period, the privatized firms carry higher debt levels than their counterparts. However, because of the significant improvement in profitability, their ability to service the debt has improved quite markedly in the post-privatization period. The interest coverage ratio has improved from 0.29 times to a reasonable level of 2.44 times two years after privatization (the rule of thumb is that an interest coverage ratio of 2 times is appropriate).

The privatization and the attendant change in the objective of the firm to profit maximization has also led to a significant attrition in staff levels, especially in the year following the year of privatization. The reduction in staff level of 6.44% by the privatized firms one year after privatization is significantly different from the increase in staff level of 2% observed for the industry counterparts. In the three years following the privatization, the privatized firms reduced employment by 1.74%, while their counterparts increased staff levels by 8.42%, thus generating a statistically significant industry adjusted reduction in staff levels of about 10%. The finding that the privatized firms reduced employment levels subsequent to privatization is consistent with the evidence documented in Ramamurti (1997), LaPorta and Lopez-de-Silanes (1999), Dewenter and Malatesta (2001), and Otchere and Chan (2003) and Otchere (2005). This evidence is, however, contrary to the findings of Megginson et al (1994) and Boubakri and Cosset (1998) who find evidence of increase in employment levels following privatization.

Pelican (1993) argues that under private (and tradable ownership) the search for competent owners never stops, while under government ownership, all such effort is blocked regardless of how good or bad the manager proves to be. Villalonga (2000) also suggests that there is a transition period of low operating performance inherent in any privatization process because of organizational inertia encountered by the newly privatized firms' management which results in part from initial resistance to change. The implication of the foregoing argument is that privatized firms may not show efficiency improvements immediately after privatization, but as the initial resistance to change is overcome, the privatized firms may exhibit an increasing trend in the evolution of its post privatization efficiency. Contrary to the organizational inertial conjecture however, we find that our sample firms' performance improves in the years immediately following the privatization. This improvement could be due to the corporatization of the firms prior to privatization. Corporatization involves the state-owned enterprises being maintained under public ownership while at the same time they are required to achieve certain commercial benchmarks, pay tax, borrow funds without government guarantee and lose any regulatory advantages they had. Some of these firms operated on commercial terms prior to privatization.

In summary, the evidence presented in Table 4 clearly shows that the privatized firms have become more profitable than their industry counterparts but their operating efficiency has not significantly improved. The improvement in profitability ratios thus appears to have come from increase in revenue. The evidence relating to operating performance documented in this study is consistent with the findings reported by Megginson et al. (1994) and D'Souza et al. (2000)). Megginson et al. (1994) suggest that capital market monitoring that accompanies privatization elicits post-privatization performance improvements. Holstrom and Tirole (1995) also suggest that the benefits from capital market monitoring depend on the level of sophistication of the market and the intensity of the monitoring provided by investors and analysts. Consistent with this assertion, Otchere (2005) finds that privatized firms in middle and low income countries do not perform as well as their private counterparts and attributes his findings, among others, to the fact that privatized firms in these countries face less capital market monitoring since shareholders have less access to information and also lack the power to sanction managerial performance. Consequently, privatized firm that operate in less developed capital markets may not be as aggressive as their counterparts in well-developed and active capital market such as the Australian capital market and may therefore not restructure their operations to improve performance.

4.3. Political Economy of Privatization: Federal (Commonwealth) vs. State Government Privatizations

Prior studies have suggested that conservative governments are more prone to privatization than governments with more socialist or populist orientation. For example, Sciniscalco et al. (2001) suggest that large scale privatization programs have been associated with the leadership of right wing governments (including the Thatcher government of the UK). These 'right-leaning' market-oriented politicians choose to privatize by allocating substantial amount of shares of the privatized firms to the middle class and thus creating a form of popular capitalism and a constituency of voters interested in maximizing the value of their wealth (Bias and Perotti, 2001). Thus privatization and the allocation of shares to the citizens at a discount becomes a by-product of a forward-looking opportunistic behavior of gaining future support from constituencies of the shareholders of the privatized firms. These market-oriented politicians are also seen as being capable of marshalling support of investors and are able to restrain any policy reversals, both of which can affect the performance of the privatized firms. While in Australia privatization has been carried out by both the Liberal and Labour governments at the Federal (Commonwealth government) level, the small sample size precludes a worthwhile analysis of the performance of the privatized firms along the liberal-labour (market oriented-populist) government dichotomy. In this section we examine whether the market effects observed for the sample firms depend on whether the privatization was undertaken by the Federal (Commonwealth) or State government since the Commonwealth governments may have more credibility and reputation in the market place and may be able to marshal support of private investors. We do so by examining investors' *expectation* of the performance and the *actual* performance of firms privatized by the Federal (Commonwealth) and State governments.

Privatization occurs partly because governments want to improve the efficiency and competitiveness of the privatized firms. Since there is no stock market data on the privatized firms at the time of the privatization announcement, it is not possible to determine investors' reaction to the privatization announcement regarding the expected gains in efficiency and competitiveness of the privatized firms. However, Eckel et al. (1997) argue that the stock market's expectation of the efficiency of the privatized firm can be inferred from changes in

Table 5. Federal (Commonwealth) vs. State Government privatizations

This table presents the result of the stock market effects and the operating performance of firms privatized by the Federal (Commonwealth) government and State governments. Panel A shows the stock market reaction of industry counterparts to the privatizations announced by the Federal (Commonwealth) and State governments. Panel B shows the long run performance of the privatized firms and their industry counterparts whereas Panel C shows the industry adjusted performance of the firms privatized by the Federal (Commonwealth) and State governments. The figures in parentheses are t-statistics and the symbol ***, **, * indicates significance at the 1%, 5% and 10% level respectively.

Panel A. Daily abnormal returns of rivals of firms privatized by the Commonwealth and State Governments

Event days	Rivals of firms privatized by the Commonwealth Government (N=79)		Rivals of firms privatized by State Governments (N=48)		Difference	
	% Return	t-statistic	% Return	t-statistic	Return	t-statistic
[-5, 5]	-2.00	-2.23**	2.69	2.66**	4.69	-3.21***
[-2, 2]	-1.13	-1.90**	-0.60	-0.57	-0.53	-0.66
[-1, 1]	-1.58	-3.41***	-0.22	-0.25	-1.36	-0.90
[-1, 0]	-1.39	-3.65***	0.27	0.44	-1.83	-1.77*
[0]	-0.59	-2.29**	-0.21	-0.57	-0.38	-0.71
[0, 2]	-0.43	-0.93	-1.29	-1.56	0.86	0.29
[0, 5]	-1.48	-2.38**	0.58	0.87	-2.06	-2.31**

Panel B. Distribution of sample firms' three-year cumulative abnormal returns of firms privatized by the Commonwealth and State Governments and those of their rivals following the privatization announcement

Months	Privatized Firms (N=13)			Rivals (N=127)		
	Commonwealth	State	Difference	Commonwealth	State	Difference
[1, 12]	3.70	12.69	-8.99	-22.75	-7.16	-15.59
	(0.38)	(3.18)**	(-0.84)	(2.21)	(1.19)	(-1.31)
[1, 24]	24.38	9.44	14.94	-40.80	2.72	-43.52
	(1.86)	(1.86)	(0.90)	(2.23)	(0.22)	(-1.95)*
[1, 36]	21.45	18.17	3.28	-30.42	-7.46	-22.96
	(1.59)	(1.59)	(0.19)	(1.54)	(0.58)	(-0.97)

Panel C. Difference in privatized firms' returns and the rival firms' returns

	Privatization by Commonwealth Government (Privatized – rivals)		Privatization by State Government (Privatized – rivals)	
	% Difference	t-statistic	% Difference	t-statistic
[1, 12]	26.45	1.89**	19.85	2.75***
[1, 24]	65.18	2.89***	6.72	0.42
[1, 36]	51.87	2.17**	25.63	1.49

the rival firms' stock price following the privatization announcement. Based on this assertion, we present in Table 5 evidence of the market reaction of the industry counterparts and the long run stock market performance of the privatized firms. Panel A presents the industry counterparts' reaction to privatizations announced by the Federal (Commonwealth) and State governments. Panel B shows the long run cumulative abnormal returns for the firms privatized by both the Commonwealth and State Governments, and Panel C presents the differences in abnormal returns earned by the sample firms stratified along the Federal (Commonwealth) -State government dichotomy.

We observe that the industry counterparts' reaction to privatization announcements made by the Federal (Commonwealth) government is much stronger than the reaction of rivals to privatizations announced by the State governments. Whereas the rivals' abnormal returns for the different event windows are negative and mostly significant for Federal (Commonwealth) government privatizations, those announced by State governments did not elicit strongly negative abnormal returns from industry counterparts. Since Governments of Australia do not abrogate the commitments made by previous governments, the observed differential reaction of the industry counterparts could reflect size effects. Firms privatized by the Federal (Commonwealth) government tend to be larger than those privatized by State governments. Using proceeds from the share issue privatization as a proxy for size, we note that the proceeds from the first and second tranche of Telstra's share issue privatizations that accrued to the Federal (Commonwealth) government are much larger than the combined proceeds realized by the State governments from the privatization of state assets (see Table 1). From the perspective of this study, this is an important feature because such large privatization offerings generate significant intra-industry effects on industry counterparts.

It can be inferred from these results that investors *expected* that the privatization of large national icons such as the Commonwealth Bank of Australia and Telstra will lead to better performance for the privatized firms and that these privatization will affect the competitive position of the industry counterparts. In terms of the *actual* performance, we find that the long run market-adjusted performance of the Federal (Commonwealth) Government's share issue privatizations appears to be economically and statistically better than that of the firms privatized by State governments. However, the difference is not statistically significant, although in the first year, the firms privatized by the State governments outperformed those privatized by the Federal (Commonwealth) Government. On a relative basis, we note that the industry-adjusted abnormal returns realized by firms privatized by the Federal (Commonwealth) Governments are better than those realized by their industry counterparts' on both economic and statistical grounds. As the results presented in Panel C show, firms privatized by state governments outperformed their industry counterparts, however, only year 1 results are statistically significant.

5. Summary and Conclusion

In this paper, we take stock of the operating and stock market performance of share issue privatizations in Australia, a country whose privatization program ranks second among the OECD countries in terms of the relative size of GDP. Based on the assertion that investors expect privatization to significantly impact on industry counterparts through industrial repositioning, we find that the industry counterparts reacted negatively to the privatization announcements. We find that in the three years following privatization, the privatized firms outperform the market index and the industry counterparts. Also, firms privatized by the Federal (Commonwealth) Government had significant market effects than those privatized by State Governments.

In terms operating performance, we find that the privatized firms have become more profitable in the post-privatization period than in the pre-privatization period, but their operating efficiency has not significantly improved. The improvement in profitability thus appears to have come from increase in revenue. Focusing on the yearly median ratios, we document an upward trend in all the profitability measures of the privatized firms. On a relative basis we observe that the privatized firms have become more profitable than their industry counterparts. However, they have been less efficient than their rivals in reducing expenses. The privatization and the attendant change in the objective of the firm to profit maximization have also led to a significant attrition in staff levels. Even after controlling for contemporaneous economy-wide factors, we find that share issue privatization in Australia has yielded significant stock market and operating performance improvements.

Appendix 1: Ratios

Measures	Ratios	Calculation
Profitability	Profit Margin (PM)	Net Income /Net Sales
	Return on Asset (ROA)	Net Income/Total Assets
	Return on Equity (ROE)	Net Income/Total Equity
	Return on Cash Flows (ROCF)	(EBIT + Depreciation)/Total Assets
Operating Efficiency	Expense/Income Ratio (TETR)	Total Operating Expenses/Total Revenue
Asset Efficiency	Asset Turnover (ATO)	Net Sales/Total Assets
Capital Expenditure	Capital Investment Spending (CE)	Capital Expenditures/Net Sales
	Capital Expenditure Growth Rate (GCE)	Capital Expenditures(t)/ Capital Expenditures (t-1)-1
Leverage	Debt to Asset Ratio (DA)	Total Liabilities/Total Assets
	Interest Cover Ratio (IC)	EBIT/Interest Expense
Employment	Employment growth rate (ΔLAB)	(No. of employees (t)/No. of employees (t-1)) -1

References

Aggarwal, R, R. Leal and L. Hermandez, 1993, The aftermarket performance of initial public offerings in Latin America, *Financial Management* **22**, 43-53.

Boubakri N., and J. Cosset, 1998, The financial and operating performance of newly privatized firms: Evidence from developing countries, *Journal of Finance* **53**, 1081-1110.

Bortolotti B, M. Fantini and C. Scarpa, 2000, Why do governments sell privatized companies abroad, Working paper, Fondazione Eni Enrico Mattei, Milan, Italy.

Boycko, M., A. Shleifer and R. W. Vishny, 1996, A theory of privatization, *Economic Journal* **106**, 309-319.

Dewenter, K., and Malatesta, P.H., 2001 State-owned and privately owned firms: an empirical analysis of profitability, leverage, and labor intensity. *American Economic Review* **91**, 320-334.

D'Souza, J, W. Megginson and R. Nash, 2000, Determinants of performance improvements in privatized firms: The role of restructuring and corporate governance, *Working paper*, University of Oklahoma.

Eckel, C., D. Eckel, and V. Singal, 1997, Privatization and efficiency: Industry effects of the sale of British Airways, *Journal of Financial Economics* **43**, 275-298.

Galal, A., L. Jones, P. Tandon, and I. Vogelsang, 1994, Welfare consequences of selling public enterprises, The World Bank, Washington D.C.

Jones, S., W. Megginson, R. Nash and J. Netter, 1999, Share issue privatizations as financial means to political ends, *Journal of Financial Economics*, **53**, 217-53

LaPorta, R., and Lopez-de-Silanes, F., 1999, The benefits of privatization: evidence from Mexico, *Quarterly Journal of Economics* **114**, 1193-1242.

Lee, P., Steiner N., Taylor, S and Walter, T., 2002, Australian Share Issue Privatization: Balancing finance and politics, *Working paper,* University of Technology, Sydney.

Levis, M., 1993. The long-run performance of initial public offerings: The UK experience 1980-1988, *Financial Management* **22**, 28-41.

Megginson, W. L., R. C. Nash, and M. van Randenborgh, 1994, The financial and operating performance of newly privatized firms: An international empirical analysis, *Journal of Finance* **49**, 403-452.

Megginson, W. L., and J. M Netter, 1998, From state to market: A survey of empirical studies on privatization, *Journal of Economic Literature*, **39** 321-389.

Menyah, K and K. Paudyal, 1996, Share issue privatization: The UK experience, in Mario Levis (ed), Empirical Issues in Raising Equity Capital (Elsevier Science, Amsterdam).

Omran, M., 2002. Initial and aftermarket performance of Egyptian Share Issue Privatization, *Working Paper,* Arab Monetary Fund, Economic Policy Institute, Abu Dubai, UAE.

Otchere, I., 2005. Do privatized banks in middle and low-income countries perform better than rival banks? An intra-industry analysis of bank privatization, *Journal of Banking and Finance* **29**, 2067-2093.

Otchere, I., and J. Chan, 2003. Intra-industry effects of bank privatization: A clinical analysis of the privatization of the Commonwealth Bank of Australia, *Journal of Banking and Finance,* **27**, 949 – 975.

Pelican, P., (1993), Ownership of firms and efficiency: the competence argument, *Constitutional Political Economy* **4**, (3a) 349-392

Perotti, E.C., 1995, Credible privatization, *American Economic Review* **85**, 847-859.

Perotti, E and van Oijen, P., 2001, Privatization, market development, and political risk in emerging economies, *Journal of International Money and Finance* **20**, 43-69.

Ramamurti, R., 1997, Testing the limits of privatization: Argentine Railroads, *World Development* **25**, 1973-1993

Reserve Bank of Australia, 1997, Australia's privatization program.

Shleifer, A and R. Vishny, 1994, Politicians and firm, *Quarterly Journal of Economics*, **109**, 995-1025.

Siniscalco, D., Bortolotti B, M. and Fantini, 2001, Privatization around the world: New evidence from panel data, *working paper*, Fondazione Eni Enrico Mattei, Milan, Italy.

Subrahmanyam A., and S. Titman, 1999, The going-public decision and the development of financial markets, *Journal of Finance*, **54**, 1045-1082.

Sun, Q., and W.H.S Tong, 2003, China share issue privatization: the extent of its success, *Journal of Financial Economics*, **70**, 183-222

Vickers, J. and G. Yarrow, 1989, *Privatization: An Economic Analysis*. Cambridge: MIT Press.

Villalonga, B., (2000), Privatization and efficiency: differentiating ownership from political, organizational, and dynamic effects, *Journal of Economic Behavior and Organisation* **42**, 43-74.

Verbrugge, J. A., W. L., Megginson, and W. Lee, 1999. The financial performance of privatized banks: an empirical analysis, *Working paper* (University of Georgia).

In: Global Privatization and Its Impact
Editors: I.J. Hagen and T.S. Halvorsen, pp. 47-59

ISBN: 978-1-60456-785-4
© 2008 Nova Science Publishers, Inc.

Chapter 3

PRIVATIZATION, LAND MARKET AND LAND USE CONVERSION IN CHINA

K.W. Chau and Winky K.O. Ho[*]

Department of Real Estate and Construction, University of Hong Kong

Abstract

The liberalization of the land use market has become the most pressing economic issue for the Chinese Government in recent years. The objective of this paper is to provide an overview of land market operations in China with an update of its land policies. It will first present some background information about the establishment of the land market and its transformation, and then document the land development process in China. The foregoing section discusses the problems associated with land acquisitions and how the Chinese Government has tried to overcome them, especially the loss of agricultural land due to its conversion from agricultural to non-agricultural uses, and the disputes between farmers and governments. The last section will offer a summary of this paper.

1. Introduction

Modern China has become an increasingly urbanized and industrialized country that has experienced substantial economic growth and rapid urbanization over the last 20 years. Per-capita GDP rose sharply from ¥381 in 1978 to ¥1,519 in 1989, and expanded thereafter to ¥14,040 by 2005, which was an average annual growth rate of 13.75% over 28 years. Population increased at an average annual rate of 1.10% during the same period, totaling 1,307.56 million in 2005 while the number of households grew from 206.41 million to 360.9 million during 1978-2003 period, at an annual growth rate of 2.17% over 26 years. Rapid urbanization took place most notably in Beijing and the eastern coastal cities, such as Shanghai, Guangzhou, and Shenzhen. China accommodates one-fifth of the world's population and Chinese real estate markets are still in a state of evolution. In fact, experts

---

[*] E-mail address: winkyho@hkucc.hku.hk. Fax: (852) 2559 9457, Dr. Winky K.O. Ho, Department of Real Estate and Construction, 5/F., Knowles Building, University of Hong Kong, Pokfulam Road, Hong Kong.

predict that they will comprise one-fifth of the world's real estate markets when they are fully developed (Zhao et al., 1999). China's territory of 9.6 million km² consists of 31 provinces, autonomous regions, and municipalities. The built-up area constitutes around 32.6% (313.33 million hectares) of all land, with 13.5% (130.04 million hectares) used for cultivation, and 11.3% (108 million hectares) still undeveloped (China Statistical Yearbook, 2006). The rest of the country is mainly composed of usable agricultural land (35.35 million hectares), afforested land (284.93 million hectares), undeveloped land for usable afforestation (54.71 million hectares), and grassland (400 million hectares).

2. Land Use System

In post-war China, housing construction was classified as "non-productive" investment, and thus, given fewer resources than other capital investments (Chen, 1998). There was virtually no trading of private or public housing before its economic reforms in 1980. Public housing construction was facilitated primarily through the appropriation of Central Government funds that were allocated to local governments and state enterprises (SOEs) for building rental apartments. Then these rental units were allocated to the employees of SOEs and government offices at nominal rents under the "low income and low expenditures" policy constituted during the establishment of the socialist economy. Under this system, governments would collect implicit income taxes by offering low wages to workers first, and then subsidize them in the form of housing, food, medical care provisions, etc. Most people in urban China had lived under the welfare housing system in which the government provided nearly free housing for urban residents. All government agency, academic and public institution, and SOEs employees were allocated housing from the government or their work units.

Since the open-door policy was implemented in the early 1980s, China's transitional economy has undergone significant economic, political, and social transformation. Economic inefficiency that resulted from the existing resource allocation mechanism became more visible. This land policy and "low income and low expenditure policy" had many drawbacks: (i) housing rent had remained more or less intact before 1982, comprising less than 1 percent of urban residents' annual salary or expenditure, and did not even cover construction costs, management, maintenance, depreciation, etc.; (ii) low housing rents led to severe housing shortage in urban areas; (iii) housing allocation by the bureaucratic system gave rise to corruption among government officials; and (iv) people were reluctant to move as they were tied to their low-rent housing units, which posed a barricade to the restructuring and relocation of the enterprises.

Although the 1982 constitutional regulations on land failed to interpret the distinction between land use rights and ownership, the government carried out the process of transformation. This was most visible in the urban areas of the eastern coastal cities. This fundamental economic and social transformation involved the transfer of existing real estate stock, especially housing, from the states and municipalities to individuals and private firms through market and/or quasi-market transactions. This type of economic behavior gradually formed a real estate market that encompasses all transactions involving a transfer of rights or interests in land and buildings from one party to another, temporarily or permanently, in return for a consideration. Privatization has been introduced into every aspect of the Chinese economy. Commodity markets, together with factor markets, have been gradually established in response to the strong inclination of economic development.

In September 1987, China again gained the extensive attention of the international forum, both politically and economically, when the Shenzhen Municipal Government zones first began to experiment with land lease contract. A local company received a plot of land for a lease of 50 years. In 1988, the China's Constitution was amended again to establish a framework for distinguishing land use rights from land ownership. It clearly states: "Land use can be transferred according to the law". In the Temporary Regulations for State-Owned Urban Land Use Right Conveyances and Transfers, published in May 1990, Chinese law formally recognized that use rights of state-owned urban land are independent economic rights. Within a time limit, usually 50 years for industrial use, 40 years for commercial use, and 70 years for residential use, these rights can be sold, exchanged, bestowed as a gift, leased, and used for mortgages. Under the tax reforms introduced in 1994 and implemented in 1995, the transfer of these property rights was subject to a land value-added tax with rates ranging from 30-60 percent (Keng, 1996).

In March 1998, Premier Zhu Rongji introduced a new package of reforms that included a series of housing reforms with an intention to stimulate the domestic economy. Subsidized housing traditionally available to Chinese workers would be phased out, while workers would be encouraged to buy their own homes or pay rents closer to market prices. The reforms called for workers to use their savings, alongside the once-and-for-all housing subsidies they received, to purchase their own homes. In August 1999, the government announced that all vacant residential housing units built after January 1, 1999 would be sold rather than allocated. Since then, the private residential property market has experienced tremendous growth. Under the new constitution, a rough framework of China's real estate market has gradually emerged.

3. Land Development Process

In China, where there is no absolute ownership of urban land other than by the government, land in the suburban areas and countryside is collectively owned, unless otherwise specified. Under this jurisdiction, a real estate transaction merely involves a transfer of land rights, but not a transfer of its absolute ownership per se, as this remains under the sovereignty of the state within whose frontiers it lies. The term "leasehold" has been widely understood in that it describes an exclusive occupation right of land with an expiry date and periodic payments to a higher landlord.

In the urban land market, land use rights fall under two sectors, the urban-state and urban-commercial sectors, which can be assigned two ways. Allocation is to dispose of land use rights to SOEs or non-profit making organizations with no expiry date, while conveyance disposes of the rights to profit-making enterprises/commercial users with an expiry date. The primary land market (*yiji shichang*) transactions are processed by these two methods. State allocations are transacted at allocation prices that consist of (i) the expropriation cost of land (*zhengdi fei*, the cost of transferring the ownership status from collective form to state ownership); (ii) various stipulated land fees (*tudi guifei*) and; (iii) allocation fees set by the government (*huabo fei*).

State conveyance is transacted at a conveyance price that is composed of (i) and (ii) described above and; (iii) the conveyance fees (*churang jin*). The last component is determined by negotiation (*xieyi*), auction (*paimai*) or public tender (*zhaobiao*). In addition, the government will levy fees to cover the development cost (*kaife fei*) if it has previously invested in infrastructure construction. Generally speaking, conveyance fees are determined by market forces so that they would be much higher than the allocation fees. In other word, commercial land users, unlike SOEs, obtain land lots at much higher cost and with expiry dates. From 1993-1998, there were 574,231 hectares of urban land transacted by allocation and 245,968 hectares of urban land transacted by conveyance in the primary market (Ho and Lin, 2003).

Although profit-making enterprises obtain land by conveyance at a higher cost, they are eligible to participate in the secondary land market (*erji shichang*) by (i) transferring (*zhuanrang*) the land use rights to other parties, (ii) renting the rights (*chuzu*), and (iii) making use of the rights as collateral (*diyi*). These three transaction modes together are described as circulation (*liuzhuan*). On the one hand, the "resale" of land use rights enables the rights holder to make a profit as the land price in the secondary market is well above the conveyance price in the primary market. On the other hand, the rights of putting the land use rights as collateral are crucial to the private enterprise's operation and financial management, in respect of the immature capital markets and negative bank lending attitude towards lending without collateral. During 1993-1998, there were 1,427,585 hectares of urban land that were transferred, leased and mortgaged (Ho and Lin, 2003).

The right to participate in the secondary land market does not apply to enterprises that obtain land rights by allocation. However, it is possible to re-allocate land from state use to commercial use by compensating the difference between the allocation price and conveyance price. Cities, acting as agents of the State, can acquire land back from SOEs by paying them compensation fees (including demolition fee, *chaiqian fei*), and then reselling the land lot to private enterprise by conveyance. SOEs can engage in transactions in the secondary market, however, as long as they pay a conveyance fee for the land they have obtained through allocation if they change to private ownership. While transactions of land use rights are prohibited among SOEs, exchange of land use rights among them are allowed, providing that the transaction are registered and the involved parties that receive benefits from an appreciation in land values, pay compensation consisting of stipulated fees and appreciation taxes (*tudi zhangzhi shui*). In reality, this exchange of land among SOEs is infrequent, but it offers another channel for land to be circulated within the urban-state sector.

In April 2002, the Ministry of Land and Resources (MLR) issued a regulation Document No. 11 to prohibit the land use right transfers by mutual agreements. Starting from July 1, 2002, any procurement of land for business purposes, including commercial, tourism, entertainment and commercial residence, can only be carried out through market transaction, such as bidding, auction and listing on authorized exchange platforms. To be consistent with regional and national policies, many local governments have adopted similar rules. In June 2002, the Beijing municipal government issued a notice to abandon most transfers of land use rights for business use by mutual agreements with the exceptions of construction projects in towns and small cities and land use for high-tech industries.

In January 2004, the Beijing government again promulgated the No. 4 Decree, which removed these exceptions. However, it is inapplicable to those agreement-based land use transfers that had already been approved by the government before the dates of their issue.

Some provinces, such as Yunnan, followed Beijing's step in enforcing the land bidding and listing procedures. To guarantee the success of Document No. 11, the MLR promulgated Document No. 71, which stipulates that land owners who obtain land use rights by agreement must obtain land use certificates and development licenses by August 31, 2004. Also, developments must commence within 2 years after a land sale. If a landowner fails to comply with this regulation, his/her land lots will be requisitioned and put on the market again through auction or tender (*People's Daily*, 25 August 2004).

Furthermore, in August 2003, the State Council issued a notice to emphasize that land supply must be strictly controlled and the approval authority for land grants shall not be assigned to the government at a level lower than that of a provincial government. In preserving cultivated land, the amount of which had fallen from 130.1 million hectare in 1996 to 123.5 million hectares by the end of 2003 (*China Daily*, 2004), the MLR called for the stricter monitoring of land use authorizations by suspending the approval of new applications for construction projects in cities that failed to report their land use situations between 1999 and 2004 by the January 15, 2004 deadline. In 2004, 26 out of 84 Chinese cities, including Beijing, failed to submit their land use reports on time. Local governments that submit fraudulent reports should expect even more severe punishment. The MLR used satellite remote sensors to help ensure the accuracy of the reports.

3.1. Land Sales Application System

In China, land development is a very complicated and lengthy process. For economic efficiency purposes, land is usually developed in a comprehensive way, rather than piecemeal. Under the existing land use system, comprehensive land development (for example, a large residential development, together with recreational facilities and infrastructure, etc.) is largely initiated by the government within whose frontiers it lies. To participate in the land development business, private developers, either local or foreign, must fully understand how to get their development proposals through to all the relevant government departments and authorities in order to obtain land use rights. Good connections with government officials are also essential.

Under the land sale application system, city and provincial governments can announce a list of sites available for sale upon application. The application list contains information about location, site area, use, and the estimated availability date of each land lot, etc. Typically, interested parties must submit an application form, together with a deposit, to the relevant government departments. An alternative way for private developers to obtain land is to submit a development project proposal to the relevant government agency with a definition of its purpose, requirements, and general aspects, such as location, scope and layout. The definition and planning of the project must be carried out in coordination with the government agency in charge, such as provincial, municipal, and autonomous region governments, as well as central ministries or commissions. The priority projects are subject to review and approval by the State Council.

The review and approval procedure checks if a project complies with the national economic and social programs, and if the enterprise is resourceful enough to complete the project on schedule. Once the proposal is approved, the enterprise is required to submit its site choice and feasibility reports that identify the risks involved. Various factors, such as climate, topographical and geological conditions, transport, and environmental impact, should be considered when the enterprise selects a site for development and prepares its feasibility report. To maximize its chances of a successful application, an enterprise will usually submit several development proposals for review and government agents will evaluate them with respect to the above factors. All potential sites will be examined to see if they are suitable for the pre-determined types of development, and whether these proposed developments violate the planning requirements. Site choice and feasibility reports also need to be submitted to the appropriate planning authority for review and approval. As for priority projects, their reports have to be submitted to the State Council. Once they are approved by the relevant government agency or planning authorities, the development project will be listed in the government's annual development time schedule and the enterprise can seek to obtain the land use rights.

According to the 1990 Assignment and Transfer of Use Rights of State Owned Land in Urban Areas Temporary Regulation, other than through negotiation, private developers can obtain land by bidding at land auctions or through government tenders (Regulation 13). Forming a joint venture with a local enterprise is also a feasible way for foreign enterprises (including Hong Kong, Taiwan and Macau-based enterprises) to obtain land. All land transactions are managed by the State Land Administration Bureau (SLAB, *guojia tudi guanli ju*). If a developer is successful in winning a land use right, it should sign an assignment of the use rights of land with the Lands Department under the SLAB and pay 10% of the conveyance price on the date it signs the contract and the rest within the next 59 days. After paying the land price and relevant tax payment in full, the developers should register with the Land Registry to obtain the land use right within 30 days from the date it settles payment. Once it obtains the land use right, the developer can get the piece of land back, demolish any unwanted structures, and start the surveying works. However, it cannot start building on the land until it obtains the construction and commence work permits from the Planning Department and the Construction Department.

3.2. Sales of Real Estate

Generally speaking, a private developer can apply to the Real Estate Management Bureau (*fangdi chan guanli ju*) to sell dwelling units through pre-sales. An application will more likely be approved if the following requirements are fulfilled: (i) developers must pay all the fees for their land-use rights and obtained certificates for their land-use rights; (ii) developers must have permits for construction project planning; (iii) each construction project must comprise at least 25 percent of the total investment, computed on the basis of the commercial houses provided for pre-sale; (iv) the schedule of construction and completion dates must be set; (v) developers must make registrations for a pre-sale with the respective governmental departments at or above the county level and obtain certificates of permission for the pre-sale of commercial houses; and (vi) the proceeds obtained from the pre-sale of commercial houses must be invested in their respective construction projects (Liaoning Sun-Land Law Firm). Foreign-based developers usually sell their units through property agents because they lack experience and an understanding of local conditions.

In the presence of prevailing high property prices, the government has tried to cool down the real estate market by tightening the pre-sale restrictions. In April 2003, the Supreme People's Court ruled that it was illegal to execute a sales contract before a developer has obtained a pre-sale permit, and developers who violate this regulation would be fined and the Department of Land Administration under the government at a county level or above would confiscate the proceeds of their unlawful transactions. To recoup capital quickly, many developers, however, have sold their properties through pre-sales without getting approval from the government, which violates Article 44 of the Law of the People's Republic of China on Administration of the Urban Real Estate. Figures from the Ministry of Construction revealed that more than 80 percent of residential properties were sold by pre-sales in major Chinese cities, with the figure exceeding 90 percent in some cities (China Economic Information Network, 26 August 2005). Although the price of residential properties sold by pre-sales is usually set 10-15 percent lower than those for completed properties, this pricing arrangement allows developers to recoup their capital 10 months earlier and replenish their cash flows quickly. Unanimously, developers find it hard to resist selling properties through pre-sales, and it seems that the tightening of the restrictions has been unable to suppress the property market.

3.3. Restrictions on Foreign Buyers

In July 2006, six ministries led by the Ministry of Construction issued a statement requiring foreigners to live in China for at least a year before being allowed to buy a house (Moxley, 2007). This regulation is also applicable to overseas residents, including those from Hong Kong and Macao Special Administrative Regions, Taiwan Province and Chinese living abroad. However, it was just a verbal statement that was not enforced, so property developers in the capital once again started accepting subscriptions from foreign buyers. In January 2008, a new rule required foreigners living in Beijing to obtain certificates from the Beijing Municipal Public Security Bureau to prove that they have been in China for at least one year for work or study before being allowed to buy property. Each prospective foreign buyer had to produce a passport and documents to prove the length of time they have spent working or studying in Beijing, papers verifying his/her present address, and two passport-sized photos. Overseas residents also had to submit a signed testimony, declaring that s/he would occupy the property. In supplement, the rule restricted foreigners from buying more than one house or using it for non-residential purposes.

4. Land Use Conversion

The 1978 Constitution of the People's Republic of China (amended in 1993) authorized the compulsory acquisition or resumption of land[1] by the government. Article 10 of the Chinese Constitution states that "[the] state may, in the public interest, requisition land for its use in accordance with the law." In China, compulsory land acquisitions are known as 'zhengdi.' As land occupiers do not own the land, all compulsory land acquisitions in China are actually "compulsory land resumptions" in which only land use rights and all structures on the land are requisitioned by the acquiring authority, which legitimates compensations to the landowners or occupants. Under the authority of the Constitution, there are separate laws

---

[1] As the land leasehold system is adopted in China, land acquisition and land resumption are interchangeably used in this chapter.

governing the acquisition of farmland and urban land. Farmland may be compulsorily acquired for construction purposes under S.43 of the People's Republic of China Land Administration Law (PRCLAL), which was amended in 1998. Land cannot be acquisited until an approval for converting farmland to construction land is granted. Under S.45 of the PRCLAL, any acquisition of farmland needs prior approval, as stated in S.44 of the PRCLAL for the conversion of farmland to nonagricultural use. Furthermore, acquiring: (i) basic farmland; (ii) arable land other than basic farmland and that which is more than 35 hectares; and (iii) all other land exceeding 70 hectares requires the State Council's approval (Chan, 2003).

Urban land and buildings covered by a city plan may be compulsorily acquired under the Urban Buildings Demolition Relocation Administration Regulations of 2001 (UBDRAR) for urban development schemes. Regulation 3 of the UBDRAR requires that demolition and relocation of buildings must conform to the relevant city plan and be beneficial to urban renewal, ecological environmental improvement, and the protection of cultural relics. Under Regulation 6, demolition and relocation cannot be undertaken unless a permit has been approved by the administrative department. The unit that obtains a demolition removal permit is known as the demolition and relocation person (DRP), whereas all persons whose buildings are affected by the demolition and relocation are known as persons subject to demolition and relocation (PSDRs; Reg. 4, par. 2 & 3). The DRP and PSDRs are equivalent to the acquiring authority and dispossessed persons, respectively, in Western compensation laws (Chan, 2003).

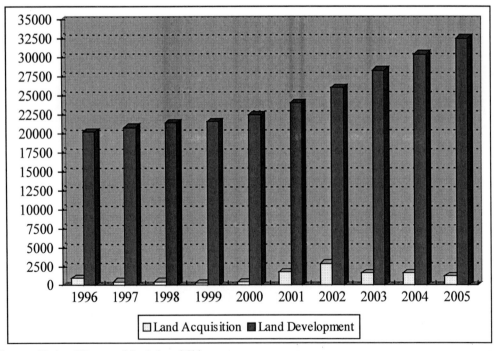

Source: National Bureau of Statistics of China.

Figure 1. Land Acquisition and Development of China (km^2).

Figure 1 presents a summary of land acquisition and development in China from 1996 to 2005. In 1996, about 1,018 km^2 of land was acquired by the government for various developments. During the 1997-2000 period, the rate of land acquisition seemed to slow. The amount of land acquisited decreased from 519 km^2 in 1997 to 447 km^2 in 2000 (National Bureau of Statistics of China, 1997-2006). However, the land acquisited has remained at very high levels since 2001, and this has been attributed to developers' incentive to generate profits in the context of price escalations in urban commodity housing. Although strict regulations governing land acquisition have been laid down, illegal acquisitions are very common in China. As GDP growth plays a crucial role in official promotions, local governments often grant illegal land use to attract investment. Surveys conducted in October 2005 and October 2006 using remote sensing satellite technology showed that 22% of new acquisitions in 90 medium-sized and large cities were illegal. More than 80% of these illegal acquisitions, totaling over 16,000 hectares, were in eight cities (*People Daily*, 27 September 2007). Zhang Xinbao, Director of the Supervision Bureau of the Ministry, announced that about 51% of new land use projects in the 90 cities were illegal and the figure was as high as 80% in 17 cities. The illegal use of land has been a growing problem in medium-sized cities, rural areas, and in Central and Western China, both of which contained the top 15 cities with the highest proportions of illegal use and acquisitions.

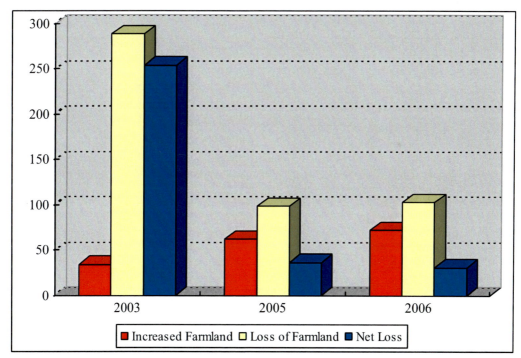

Source: National Bureau of Statistics of China.

Figure 2. Net Loss of Farmland in China (10,000 hectares).

Since a substantial amount of land acquired was farmland, the high depletion rate of farmland has alarmed top officials of the Central Government, who fear that China's loss of "self-reliance" in agriculture is fatal to its sovereignty and social stability (Ding, 2003).

Government officials announced that there were only 121.8 million hectares of farmland left, which was very close to the minimum level of 120 million hectares (300 million acres) for feeding all of China (*Agence France Presse*, 25 December 2007). Although the government has maintained stricter control over land use conversion and re-cultivated deserted land in recent years, rapid urban expansion has still caused the depletion of farmland at an unprecedented rate, particularly on the urban fringes, where the most productive land lay. For example, while there was an increase in farmland of 34.36 hectares due to the re-cultivation of deserted land in 2003, the conversion of farmland into non-agricultural use through land acquisitions amounted to 288.1 hectares, resulting in a net loss of 253.74 hectares of farmland. (see Figure 2).

On the one hand, land acquisitions have caused a drastic drop in China's farmland, which poses a threat to its food supply and social stability. On the other hand, there has been a lack of an effective compensation mechanism[2] that can head off social unrest. In recent years, mass protests in China have risen, especially over land expropriation disputes between farmers and local government officials. For example, the residents of Dongzhou Village in Guangdong's Shanwei City reported that as many as 30 people were killed during a protest on 6 December 2005 when security forces opened fire on crowds of villagers demonstrating against the construction of a coal-fired power plant in their midst. The provincial authorities acknowledged three deaths, but blamed the villagers for attacking the police. Meanwhile, Chinese authorities have restricted outside access to the village and have apparently ordered news organizations to sharply limit their coverage of the incident (French, 2006).

In another incident in Panlong (also in Guangdong) on 16 January 2006, villagers' anger had been aroused by a 2003 government land acquisition program that they originally believed was part of a construction project to build a superhighway connecting the nearby city of Zhuhai with Beijing. Later, the villagers learned the land had, in fact, been resold to developers to build special chemical and garment industries in the area. The police chased and beat protesters and bystanders, while the villagers retaliated by smashing police cars and throwing rocks at security forces in hit-and-run attacks. According to the villagers, as many as 60 people were wounded and at least one person, a 13-year-old girl, was killed by security forces in the incident (French, 2006). Then police sealed off the village and began to monitor all roads leading into the area to check identification and bar access to outsiders. News of this incident appears to have been censored within China.[3]

To solve these social problems associated with illegal land acquisition, the Central Government took action against local government officials who took bribes and promulgated judicial interpretation on Property Law on March 16, 2007 to equally protect the property of individuals, collective and that of the State. Presecutors of the Supreme People's Procuratorate (SPS) have found frequent incidences of commercial bribery in city planning, land management, and utility administration with the complicity of government officials at the local and regional levels. In the first 10 months of 2007, the government investigated 4,240 bribery cases in infrastructure and real estate projects, which accounted for 48.4 percent of total commercial bribery cases, with the consideration of 657 million yuan ($87.6 million) involved. Out of total, 3,039 involved 50,000 yuan or more. To date, prosecutors have taken

---

[2] For a detailed discussion of compensation for land acquisition in China, please see Chan (2003).

[3] Farmer protests caused by illegal land acquisitions and unreasonable compensation have occurred all across China in greater frequency recently. For example, similar incident also happened in Zhangzhuang Village of Jilin City in Shangdong Province where some villagers were injured and 7 arrested on 5 November 2006.

1,613 government officials to court, 340 of whom were officials in charge. On 13 Sepetember 2007, the National Bureau of Corruption Prevention (NBCP) was established, with Mr. Ma Wen, the Ministry of Supervision, as its head. The Bureau aims to collect and analyze information about banking, land use, medicine and telecommunication sectors, and to share it with prosecuting departments, courts and the police. On December 19, 2007, the website of the NBCP has been launched to offer a channel for the local citizens to report official corruption (*China Daily*, 20 December 2007).

As for the Property Law, it was approved by legislation in March 2007 and came into effect on October 1, 2007 after repeated revisions and eight readings. The Property Law is seen as a significant step in China's efforts to further economic reforms and boost its economy, with its Article 247 stipulating that no unit or individual may infringe upon the property of the State, the collective and the individual. On October 8, 2006, the Beijing Changping Intermediate People's Court heard the first court case involving the Property Law. The plaintiff, Mr. Shen, filed a lawsuit against the Zhongjiaxin auction house for auctioning off six apartments he bought for 1.2 million yuan from Mr. Yan in 1998 (*People.com.cn*, 2007). Yan was convicted of taking bribes in 2002 and had his property confiscated. The Intermediate People's Court of Shijiazhuang ruled that these apartments were Mr. Yan's so it allowed the auction house to hold the auction. The plaintiff requested possession of his apartments or compensation. Under the Constitution, Shen's appeal was consistent with Articles 4 and 63 of the Property Law, which ensures an individual's lawful possession of property and it inviolability. As the Property Law protects individuals' belongings by law, in the near future, more people are expected to file lawsuits with the Court when they believe their private property rights have been violated.

5. Conclusion

The liberalization of the land use market in China is in a state of transformation. On the one hand, a property developer has to comply with many complicated government laws and regulations. On the other hands, government policies frequently change, so that greater risks are associated with land development in China than in developed countries. Investors, either local or foreign, must have a clear understanding of the application procedure in order to obtain land use rights and the local business environment before entering the real estate market. This current study aims to provide some background information on the land use system, especially on China's land development process. Rapid urbanization has made parts of China more prosperous on one hand, but there remain many unresolved social problems on the other hand, such as official corruption, illegal land acquisitions, and farmers' protests. To enhance economic growth while protecting farmland, regulations and laws must be strictly enforced to streamline land acquisition, and adequate compensation must be offered to farmers who lose their land. Otherwise, the government would have only paid lip service to the citizens and uninterested in protecting individuals' belongings. In supplement, corruption among government officials sometimes allows private developers to illegally seize farmland. This corrupt practice must be halted by better enforcement of the regulations and heavier penalties.

References

Agence France Presse, (2007) Illegal land grabs in China threatening food supplies: minister, 25 December 2007.
http://afp.google.com/article/ALeqM5gAvzqlnhYITXf_E9XrDtMcMNzwZA

Chan, N. (2003) Land acguisition compensation in China – Problems & Answers. *International Real Estate Review* **6**(1): 136-152.

Chau, K.W., Ho, Winky K.O. and McKinnell, K.G. (2006) Transformation of real estate markets in transitional economies – The China experience. *State of Affairs and Development Trends in Real Estate Economy.* eds., Stephen Bone-Winkel, Wolfgang Schäfers, Matthias Thomas, Gerrit Leopoldsberger, Rolf Tilmes, Ramon Sotelo, Nico Rottke, Rudolf Müller GmbH & Co. KG, Köln, Germany, 2006: 321-340.

Chen, A.M. (1998) China's urban housing market development: problems and prospects. *Journal of Contemporary China* **7**(17): 43-50.

China Daily, (2007) Anti-corruption website crashes on first day. December 20, 2007.
http://www.chinadaily.com.cn/china/2007-12/20/content_6334343.htm

China Economic Information Network, (2005) Presale accounts for 80 percent of housing sales. August 26, 2005.
http://www1.cei.gov.cn/ce/doc/cenn/200508261461.htm

Ding, Chengri, (2003) Land policy reform in China: assessment and prospects. *Land Use Policy* **20**: 109-120.

French, H.W. (2006) Police in China battle villagers in land protest. *The New York Times*, January 19, 2006.
http://www.nytimes.com/2006/01/17/international/asia/17china.html

Ho, S.P.S. and Lin, G.C.S. (2003) Emerging land markets in rural and urban China: policies and practices. *The China Quarterly*, 681-707.

Keng, K.C.W. (1996) China's land disposition system. *Journal of Contemporary China* **5**(13): 325-345.

Liaoning Sun-Land Law Firm, Law of the People's Republic of China on administration of the urban real estate.
http://www.chinainvestlaw.com/en/content.asp?id=1027

Lichtenberg, E. and Ding, Chengri, (2008) Assessing farmland protection policy in China. *Land Use Policy* **25**: 59-68.

Moxley, M. (2007) Foreigner still hunger for Chinese real estate. *China Daily*, November 30, 2007.
http://www.chinadaily.com.cn/china/2007-10/30/content_6215204.htm

National Bureau of Statistics of China, (1997-2006) *China Statistics Yearbook 1997-2006.* Beijing: China Statistics Press.

People's Daily, (2007) Beijing court hears first case involving new Property Law. October 9, 2007.
http://english.people.com.cn/90001/90776/6279728.html

People's Daily, (2007) Over 20% of land acquisitions in China's cities illegal. September 27, 2007.
http://english.people.com.cn/90001/90778/6272123.html

Wu, J. (2008) Pressure on dwindling land banks predicted to rise again. *China Daily*, Jamuary 28, 2008.
http://chinadaily.com.cn/cndy/2008-01/31/content_6432132.htm

Zhao, Y.S. and Bourassa, S.C. (2003) China urban housing reform: recent achievements and new inequities. *Housing Studies* **18**(5): 721-744.

In: Global Privatization and Its Impact
Editors: I.J. Hagen and T.S. Halvorsen, pp. 61-85
ISBN: 978-1-60456-785-4
© 2008 Nova Science Publishers, Inc.

Chapter 4

PRIVATIZATION AS A STRATEGY OF RESTRUCTURING IN DEVELOPING ECONOMIES: THE CASE OF TURKEY

Recep Kök[1]
Department of Economics, Dokuz Eylül University, İzmir, Turkey.
Orhan Çoban[2]
Department of Economics, Selçuk University, Konya, Turkey.

Abstract

In the 1980's, the discussions and applications of privatization which began in England are still going ahead increasingly for many developed and developing countries from the beginning of 1990. Recently, privatization turned into a strategy which is preferred by developing countries for solving major economic problems or which is imposed to these countries by international organizations. It seems that the discussions about this subject are going to maintain its importance for the next years.

In this chapter, it is aimed to construct policy suggestions about how to pass from power doctrine to welfare doctrine according to privatization applications considering threats and opportunities of globalization in developing countries. Moreover, in the scope of privatization policies, dynamics of transiting from populist-voluntarist economy management to economic democracy is going to be discussed and a regulation model which can be taken as a guide for policy-makers in developing countries is going to be created based on the case of Turkey. In short, new policy suggestions are tried to be developed relating to privatization applications.

Keywords: Turkey; Regulation; Privatization; Eco-Democratic Contract Approach

1. Introduction

One of the most significant economic phenomena in recent years has been the privatization of State-Owned Enterprises (SOEs) all over the world. Whether privatization actually leads to

---

[1] E-mail address: recep.kok@deu.edu.tr. Tel: + 90 532 7231973.
[2] E-mail address: ocoban2004@hotmail.com. Tel: + 90 536 2265270; fax: + 90 384 2152010. (Corresponding Author.)

the improvement of efficiency in developing economies has been the subject of significant research studies, both theoretical and empirical. Public share in the economy has considerably increased in almost all countries due to the influence of Keynes's policies applied in the aftermath of the World War II. However, the Stagflation Crisis of the 1970s and the economic problems of this crisis have lead to the questioning of public's role in the economy. These developments have brought about the idea of privatization policies in most of the countries/regions throughout the world in the last 25 years.

In the 1980's, the discussions and practices of privatization which began in England are still going ahead increasingly for many developed and developing countries from the early 1990's. Globalization process takes some opportunities and threats for countries together and this situation forces countries to look for new strategies and policies. In this process, it can be said that countries which control "technology revolution" act as monopolizing "power doctrine" for the name of "welfare doctrine". In this conjuncture new searches for "welfare doctrine" will be sustained and potential solutions will be suggested as long as the process of privatization has not yet been completed and turned into a significant threat for developing countries. The amount of support given to industrialization strategy by privatization policies for the economical reconstruction process initiated in Turkey in 1980s is still important for Turkey and this is true for other such countries.

At that point privatization policies started to be preferred as a strategic means for restructuring economies. In addition, the debates of privatization are still continuing and various theoretical and empirical studies are performed on the effects of privatization as a policy. It will be useful to note that the consensus reached at intellectual and scientific level has a tendency towards the free market and private property proponents. The main theme of this chapter is the idea that discussions on this issue will remain important in the next years.

Privatization has the differential effects depending on the economical development levels of countries. Privatization is considered as the leading policy for the developing countries to have a sustainable development. There are some problems in developing economies in the supply of necessary capital due to insufficient capital accumulation. These countries get some financial support from international financial institutions such as the IMF and the World Bank in the form of credit and fiscal support. These institutions provide their financial supports on condition that privatization policies are maintained by these countries in accordance with economical liberalization. As a result, privatization has come to be a strategy which is implemented by the developing countries to solve their basic economical problems and/or which is imposed by the international organizations to such countries.

There is a need to establish new models in order to achieve efficient resource allocation and fair income division in developing countries in the global competition process. The handling of SOEs' with an Eco-Democratic Contract Model as it is suggested in this chapter may establish a guideline for the prevention of results of a pure free economy leading to wild capitalism and for transformation of certain challenges to certain opportunities. In this way SOEs may be restructured in a way to form the core point of a new industrialization in accordance with competitive regulation model. In short, when all the theses introduced in first part of this chapter defending SOEs' goal function and the necessity of privatization are considered "The Second Best Theorem Based Welfare Model" may become an applicable one. The Eco-Democratic Contract Model, explained here, is taken from a hypothesis which suggests that privatization has its own rationales changing in compliance with national realities and that there are rationales describing nationalization (transforming into public property) within the integrity of the same model. In this way a model, enabling establishment of mechanisms to restructure the choices of policy according to possible circumstances and combine nationalization and privatization rather than unilateral approaches pertinent to public enterprises property, has been established (Kök, 1995: 111, 209).

In this chapter, it is aimed to construct policy suggestions about how to pass from "*power doctrine*" to "*welfare doctrine*" in the context of privatization applications considering threats and opportunities of globalization in developing countries. Moreover, in the scope of privatization policies, dynamics of transitioning from populist-voluntarist economy management to economic democracy is going to be discussed and a regulation model which can be taken as a guide for policy-makers in developing countries is going to be created based on the case of Turkey. In short, new policy suggestions are developed in relation with privatization practices.

2. Economical Motivations of Privatization in Developing Economies

It can be said that the discussions on privatization will remain important in the next years when the privatization experiences in many developed and developing economies are considered. For this reason, the level of public consciousness about the main motivation and purposes of privatization is important for the implementation of effective policies particularly in developing economies.

International financial institutions such as the IMF and the World Bank started to provide financial credits to developing countries in 1970s. The risk of default in repayment of principal and interest of these credits from the early 1980s caused privatization practices to become widespread on the international platform. Special units were established within international financial institutions such as the IMF and the World Bank to spread privatization practices in order to reduce the influence of public share on economies of developing countries. As a result of activities of these units, some economic programs aiming to limit the statitism policies are put into practice in the member states for effective implementation of the IMF programs (Kök, 1995; Ghosh Banerjee and Rondinelli, 2003). In accordance with these programs, the fulfillment of duties by member countries has periodically been audited with "stand by" agreements and the countries that do their "homework" well are provided with financial support.

In the literature (Marchand et al., 1984; Ramanathan, 1986; Domberger and Piggott, 1986; Ramamurti, 1987; Perelman and Pestieau, 1988; Cremer et al., 1989; Zeckhauser and Horn, 1989; Vining and Boardman, 1992), the main objectives of SOEs in relation with the assessment of improvements in short and long term financial indicators of private enterprises are to:

- Sustain effective use of resources on the basis of coordination of economical activities and increase the competitive power of enterprises.

- Reduce income and wealth inequalities; obviate intra-regional instabilities, balance social inequalities by encouraging intra-regional development and ensuring justice.

- Create employment opportunities, provide income for state budget and maintain price stability.

- Back up skilled labour creation, improve employee wealth by improving working conditions and encourage employers' participation.

- Provide the implementation of policies which encourage import substitution.

- Make basic infrastructure investments, improve social security and provide public facilities.

- Boost foreign trade, direct the currency gain to creative fields to reduce technological dependence and thereby create a self-sufficient economy.

In summary, the main goals of public enterprises are to realize the socio-economical aims for the welfare of society and maximize the net social benefit. But the main problem here is to determine how, to what extent, why the implementation results deviate from the desired goals, and how to specify objectives precisely at the beginning.

On the other hand, there are many studies pointing out the necessity of privatization and evaluating the results of it (Megginson et al., 1994; D'Souza and Megginson, 1999; Havrylyshyn and McGettigan, 1999; Djankov and Murrell, 2000, 2002; Megginson and Netter, 2001; Kök and Çoban, 2002; Boubakri et al., 2005; Çoban and Seçme, 2005). Accordingly, it is well understood that SOEs are less effective when compared to private owned enterprises (POEs) and there are some reasons for this. Some of these reasons are; multi-dimensional goals of SOEs, type of ownership, market structure, insufficient encouragements in the management of public enterprises and bureaucratical and political interests (Boardman and Vining, 1989; Vickers and Yarrow, 1991; Laffont and Tirole, 1993; Kök, 1995; Shleifer, 1998; Havrylyshyn and McGettigan, 1999; Nellis, 1999, 2000; Djankov and Murrell, 2000, 2002; Shirley and Walsh, 2000; Sheshinski and Lopez-Calva, 2003).

In the neo-classical economic theory, the relationship between ownership structure and the efficiency of resource allocation, which is described with approaches of public choice and property rights, is explained with the changes in the nature of ownership which causes differences in the efficiency between public and private sectors. *"Public Choice and Property Rights Theory"* makes specific reference to the hypothesis which suggests ownership change will create a greater economical surplus and resource allocation will even be improved. Private ownership therefore forms the core point of the notion of sustainable activity. Consequently, it is suggested that public enterprises cannot be as efficient as private enterprises because the necessary encouragement and rewarding mechanisms doesn't work due to public ownership structure in SOEs. It is also important how and whereby the division was maintained in a specific period throughout history and the amount of effectiveness reached within that process.

One of the fundamental reasons of resource allocation inefficiency in *Public Choice Approach* is the bureaucratical structure with poor competitive conditions and auditing mechanisms which cannot be implemented in a direct way (Hayek, 1978). However, it is determined in some empirical studies on countries/sectors public enterprises that SOEs have a more efficient resource allocation. It can also be said that there is not a direct connection between the type of ownership and efficiency of resource allocation in the theoretical aspect (Saygılı ve Taymaz, 1996: 405–408; Barberis et al., 1996; Kole and Mulherin, 1997; Boubakri and Cosset, 1998, 2002; Lizal et al., 2001; Harper, 2002; Megginson et al., 2004).

On the other hand, the literature generally distinguishes two types of corporate governance mechanisms: internal and external. Internal mechanisms mainly include the organizational structure and the ownership structure of the firm, while the external mechanisms include capital market monitoring as well as the legal and institutional system. Boycko et al. (1996) developed a model to describe the relative inefficiency of SOEs and improve efficiency in the post-privatization period. According to this model, limiting state's control on economy improves the performance of firms and thus, higher profits may be achieved. On the other hand, the performance of Newly Privatized Firms is directly influenced by the increase in the amount of foreign investors in the post-privatization period. This is so because foreign investors provide new funds for newly privatized firms, create new expansions for the introduction of companies and strictly audit the activities of managers. Therefore a positive relationship is thought to exist between foreign ownership and improvement of performance in the post-privatization period. Internal monitoring mechanism is rather related to organizational structure of the firm such as the administrative board and top executive. Insufficient performance of SOEs is generally associated with the poor quality of members and managers assigned by the government. Moreover, corporate governance and monitoring mechanisms cannot be established just because of unqualified managers in the developing economies, in which corporate governance mechanisms cannot be maintained effectively and goals almost not related with profit maximization are pursued.

One of the reasons for the relative inefficiency of SOEs in developing economies is the effect of market structure on resource allocation. Some economists relate the firms' technical efficiency with competitive structure of the market and claim that it is impossible to sustain efficiency in a firm with a monopolistic structure. The sectors and firms aiming to obtain added value in global competition can increase their efficiency of resource allocation unless privatization brings about a monopolistic market structure (Kök, 1995: 22–27). The concept of dominant power has a crucial role in the explanation of public's share in the economy. In monopolistic market structures which are formed in accordance with legal regulations, the concepts of dominant power and monopolistic power have the same meaning. Economic decision units (the economic agent) which has monopolistic power in its hands (agent) – if the dominant power is a state owned enterprise, the public-, becomes a firm imposing its own regulation rather than market regulation.

The dominant or monopolistic power concepts can prevent rival or potential rival firms from entering the market, force current rivals to leave the market and complicate the diffusion and exploitation of new technologies. Such strategies bring about some economical which reduce both the efficiency of resource allocation and competition (Estache, 2001: 100). The competitive structure should therefore be improved and anti-monopolistic laws should be put into force in order to prevent misuse of monopolistic power and formations, which will reduce the efficiency of market mechanism. The notion of regulation, which is one of the main recent concerns of economy literature and shaped in accordance with the "*Regulation Theory*" of Stigler, Posner and Peltzman, has been the main point of discussions on privatization especially in developing countries. This is so because regulation is used as a means of policy to improve competitive power in international market and efficiency of resource allocation (Kök and Çoban, 2002).

What is competitive power as a concept? It would be useful to handle this issue starting from the difference between developed and developing countries since it is of crucial importance. In particular, the concepts of global and national competition should be considered at length and they should be associated with the notion of privatization in accordance with the meaning attached to them: as a matter of fact there are so many discussions in literature (Porter, 1990; Krugman, 1994; Reinert 1994; Siggel and Cockburn, 1995; Cockburn et al., 1999; Begg, 2002; Budd and Hirmis, 2004; Kitson et al., 2004; Henricsson et al., 2004; Banterle, 2005; Depperu and Cerrato, 2005). According to Haatoja and Okkonen (2004) the competitive advantage should be handled with a multidimensional approach. For example, criticizing the concept of national competitive power, Krugman (1994), suggests that this concept is a *"monomania"*. In his point of view domestic policies deviate from targets and international economical system is threatened by national competitive power. Krugman objects to the hypothesis that each country's economical future will be determined by its success in the global market. That's because, a country's commerce in the world is something different from the competition among its firms. Unlike the firms, countries aren't rivals to each other. If the term "competitive power" has a meaning, it should be explained in connection with relative productivity and competitive power at the global level. In fact each country's competitive level should be determined in accordance with its domestic productivity increase rather than the relative productivity increase on the competitive scale. According to Krugman, policies for increasing national competitive power will be hidden in a *"Mercantilism in a Lambskin Suit"* since they will only result in such things as customs protection and commercial wars (Krugman, 1994; Begg, 2002).

Mc Fedridge (1995), does not support the idea that the economical performance of a country is something different from that of firms'. According to him competitive power is shaped in compliance with objectives pertinent to performance of national economy as well as economical objectives of public policies. That's to say, competitive power and national competitive power concepts have the same meaning. On the other hand Krugman's approach which is based on productivity corresponds to United Nations approach. According to this approach not only foreign trade but also investments, technological changes and improvements and thus the dynamic improvements in the human resources are considered when determining international competitive power. In short, Krugman suggests that it is necessary to analyze competitive power at the firm and industry level. This approach is supported by Porter (1990) as well. According to Reinert (1994), who represents an alternative approach, a nation's efficiency and productivity in industrial and organizational level cannot be considered as a country's welfare indicator. In other words, a country with a low competitive power may have high competitive power on the level of firm. When viewed from the neoclassical rhetoric, welfare may be improved because productivity will increase and prices will decrease in accordance with improvements in production technology. Here national competitive power, which is analyzed under the assumptions of complete information about market, constant return to scale and equalization of factor prices becomes insignificant.

In order for the global scale competitive power to be meaningful effective policies must be developed to keep additional factor incomes inside the country. The phenomenon of imperfect competition is in the background of global competitive power. The inequality in factor prices, which is defined with imperfect competition conditions, reduces national competitive power. In conclusion, the productivity and efficiency of national firms in the micro level doesn't always mean that the national competitive power will increase. If technological developments reduce the product prices rather than increasing factor owners' (in a settled country) income, welfare improvement resulting from cost reductions parallel with productivity will be transferred to transnational consumers. Therefore national competitive power cannot be defined only with the increase in the productivity and efficiency of industry/firms.

Moreover, the relative level of national competitive power can be explained with the increase in productivity in most areas as well as policies including high quality activities resulting from information economies originated scale economies. In addition, it is necessary for the enhancement of global competitive power that national competitive power is increased. Therefore, it is of crucial importance that approaches for effective and productive use of all national resources and small scale applicable models are developed.

3. Privatization Experiences in Turkey and World

After the 1970's the function of the state in the economy have started to be questioned in many countries. At that time airline and railway transportation services as well as telecommunication, postal services, electricity, and gas services were provided by public sector. Some politicians believed that the state should go on giving service in some "strategically" important areas.

3.1. Privatization Applications in the World

After the 1970's the function of the state in the economy have started to be questioned in many countries. At that time airline and railway transportation services as well as telecommunication, postal services, electricity, and gas services were provided by public sector. Some politicians believed that the state should go on giving service in some *"strategically"* important areas.

While these discussions were going on, Thatcher government came into power in 1979 with a strong public support. Although the Thatcher government may not have launched an extensive privatization program, it adopted privatization as a major economic policy.

In the mean time, the Adenauer government in the Federal Republic of Germany launched the first large-scale, ideologically motivated "denationalization" program of the postwar era. In 1961, the German government sold a majority stake in Volkswagen in a public share offering heavily weighted in favor of small investors.

Margaret Thatcher adopted the concept of "privatization", which was originally coined to literature by Peter Drucker, instead of "denationalization" (Yergin and Stanislaw, 1998: 114). Privatization policies were strenuously attacked by the labour opposition and some enterprises sold in that process were renationalized. It was not until the successful British Telecom initial public offering in November 1984 that privatization became established as a basic economic policy in the UK. Privatization practices have gained momentum after the mid 1980's. A series of increasingly massive share issue privatizations during the last half of the 1980s and early 1990s reduced the role of SOEs in the British Economy to essentially nothing after the Tories left office in 1997, from more than 10 percent of GDP 18 years earlier. It's crucial to note that the objectives set for the Thatcher government's privatization program were virtually the same as those listed by the Adenauer government.

These goals, as described in Price Waterhouse (1989a, b), are to

- raise revenue for the state,
- promote economic efficiency,
- reduce government interference in the economy,
- promote wider share ownership,
- provide the opportunity to introduce competition and
- subject SOEs to market discipline.

The other major objective mentioned by the Thatcher government is to develop the domestic capital market by means of privatization policies directed by the government. The unexpected success of the British privatization program helped persuade many other industrialized countries to begin divesting SOEs through public share offerings. The public share in SOEs in these countries was offered to initial public offering.

Jacques Chirac's government, which came to power in France in 1986, privatized 22 companies before being ousted in 1988. The returning Socialist government did not execute any further sales, but neither did it renationalize the divested firms. Beginning in 1993, the Balladur government launched a new and even larger French privatization program, which has continued under the Jospin administration. The Socialists, in fact, launched the two largest French privatizations ever, the $7.1 billion France Telecom initial public offering in October 1997 and the subsequent $10.5 billion seasoned France Telecom issue in November 1998 (Megginson and Netter, 2001).

Several other European governments, including Italy, Germany, and Spain, also launched large privatization programs during the 1990s. These programs typically relied on public share offerings; that's the distribution of ownership to large public segments. The socialist governments didn't object to privatization practices for they have such goals to realize.

Privatization spread to the Pacific Rim, beginning in the late 1980s. Japan has sold only a relative handful of SOEs during the past 15 years, but many of these have been truly enormous. For example the three Nippon Telegraph and Telephone share offerings executed between February 1987 and October 1988 raised almost $80 billion, and in only November 1987 a public offering of $40.3 billion has been made. That remains the largest single public offering in privatization history (Megginson and Netter, 2001).

Elsewhere in Asia, governments have taken an opportunistic approach to SOE divestment. They sold pieces of large companies when market conditions are attractive. In these countries the revenues of privatization were generally used in covering budget deficits. Furthermore economic crises that gripped the region during the late 1990s have resulted in a slow down in privatization practices.

The People's Republic of China and India have taken important steps in privatization practices. The People's Republic of China launched major economic reforms as well as liberalization program in the late 1970's. These programs and reforms have enhanced the productivity of the Chinese economy. At first there have been numerous low scale privatizations, and there have been relatively few outright sales of SOEs, so the overall impact of privatization has been limited. In 1999 the government reaffirmed its commitment to privatizing the very largest state enterprises. Chinese SOEs were burdened with so many social welfare responsibilities and that the government will have difficulties in implementing a privatization program large enough to seriously undermine the state's economic role.

Another Asian country with a special position is India. It adopted a major economic reform and liberalization program in 1991, after adopting a state-directed economic development model for the first 44 years of its independence (Bai et al., 1997; Lin et al., 1998; Lin, 2000).

Latin American countries have implemented large-scale privatization practices. Particularly Chile's privatization program is remarkable. In 1990 Telefonos de Chile was privatized. In this practice of privatization they used Western capital markets and enterprise's share was sold to U.S. investors. This practice opened an important pathway for developing countries.

Mexico's, another Latin American country, privatization program was vast in scope. That country having an interventionist economic system has remarkably been successful at reducing the state's role by means of privatization. In 1982 Mexican SOEs produced 14 percent of GDP, received net transfers and subsidies equal to 12.7 percent of GDP, and accounted for 38 percent of fixed capital investment. In accordance with privatization practices, the government had privatized 361 of its 1,200 SOEs and the need for subsidies had been virtually eliminated by June 1992 (La Porta and López-de-Silanes, 1999).

Several other countries in Latin America such as Bolivia and Brasil have also executed large divestment programs. For example, Bolivia's innovative "capitalization" scheme has been widely acclaimed. However, the most important program in the region is Brazil's. Given the size of Brazil's economy and its privatization program, and the fact that the Cardoso government has been able to sell several very large SOEs in spite of significant political opposition, this country's program is likely to remain very influential. Two of these enterprises are Companhia Vale Do Rio Doce and Telebras (Megginson and Netter, 2001).

Privatization in sub-Saharan Africa has been something of a stealth economic policy. Few governments have openly adopted an explicit SOE divestment strategy, but shows that there has been substantially more privatization in the region than is commonly believed. For example in Nigeria, divesting SOEs has been repeatedly put on the agenda but there have only been some small scale divestments (Jones et al., 1999). In short privatization practices weren't successful in these countries.

The last major region to adopt privatization programs is comprised of the former Soviet-bloc countries of Central and Eastern Europe. These countries began divesting SOEs as part of a wider effort to transform themselves from command into market economies. Therefore, they faced the harsh repercussions and had a restricted set of policy choices. After the collapse of communism in 1989-91, all of the newly elected governments of the region were under pressure to create a market economy as quickly as possible. However, political considerations essentially required these governments to significantly limit foreign purchases of divested assets. Therefore governments preferred to launch "mass privatization" programs. In this divestment method shares of ownership are distributed to all citizens, usually for free or at a very low price. These programs resulted in a massive reduction of state ownership in the countries' economies. Mass privatization methods was initially popular politically, it became unpopular in many countries such as Russia. The old elite and the new oligarchs have revested their properties by various.methods. The net effects have been disappointing in some cases but have varied widely. In spite of all these disadvantages, governments in various regions have performed rapid and successful privatization practices and made great revenues by making the purchase of SOEs more appealing (Megginson and Netter, 2001).

Privatization revenues are of crucial importance in the assessment of privatization practices in developing economies. Privatization revenues in these countries are shown in the Figure-1 for the period between 1990-2005.

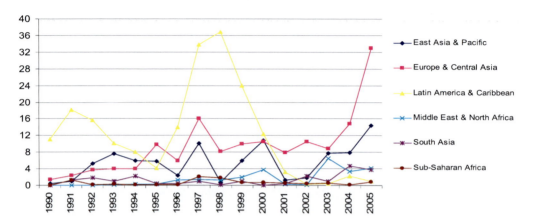

Source: World Bank, 2002, 2007; Privatization, 2007.

Figure 1. Privatization Revenues in Developing Countries, by Region, 1990–2005 ($US billions).

There was a privatization with a revenue amount of $12 billion in 1990 in developing countries and about $11 billion of this revenue came from Latin American and Caribbean counties. The revenue from the privatization in these countries gradually increased until 1997 and has reached to its peak with $65 billion in the same year. With the affect of Asia Crisis which occurred in 1997 there has been a decrease in the amount of privatization revenues after 1998. The revenue of privatization has gained momentum after 2003 and has reached to nearly $57 billion in 2005. While Latin American&Caribbean countries have obtained the highest revenues from privatization until 2000s, European and Middle Asian countries had higher amounts of revenues from privatizaion after that time (Figure-1).

The historical discussion suggests that state ownership and SOEs' share in economy have been substantially reduced since 1979. The role of SOEs in the economies of high-income (industrialized) countries has declined significantly, from about 8.5 percent of GDP in 1984 to less than 6 percent in 1991. This ratio is now thought to be below 5 percent (Sheshinski and Lopez-Calva, 2003).

The low-income countries show an even more dramatic reduction in state ownership. From a high point of almost 16 percent of GDP, the average SOEs' share of national output dropped to barely 7 percent in 1995. And it is now thought to be about 5 percent. The middle-income countries also experienced significant reductions in state ownership during the 1990s. Since the upper- and lower-middle-income groups include the transition economies of Central and Eastern Europe, this decline was expected given the extremely high beginning levels of state ownership (Megginson & Netter, 2001).

3.2. Privatization Practices in Turkey

In many developing countries public sector has been the provider of production services in industrial fields requiring a huge amount of initial investment, thus in industries involving a high level of fixed cost. The goods and services produced in such industries are provided to consumers as a state monopoly through SOEs. The reason behind the state monopoly in such markets is the natural monopoly. There are such other economical reasons as insufficient capital accumulation in private sectors, low infrastructure investments required for development, lack of collateral relations between state services and other sectors. In countries where product and services are provided by SOEs, the prices are determined either by the government or SOE governances in accordance with social objectives attached to them (Çakal, 1996: 15-17).

The status of SOEs, institutionalized with special emphasis in Turkey after the 1930's, in economy has been an important discussion point since then. The idea that SOEs can't utilize their resources as efficiently as private enterprises has become a point of manipulation because of the neo-liberalist policies after the 1980's. Turkey's economy has entered a period of restructuring after the stability program executed on Jan 24th 1980. IMF supported program has many similarities with *"Orthodox Stability Program- Orthodox Adjustment Agreement"*, which was implemented in some of Latin American countries. Being theoretically established on the basis of Neo-liberal approach, this program has the main objective of finding solutions to short term external deficit. Thus, Turkey had to agree and cooperate with international financial institutions such as the IMF and the World Bank. The program includes the following objectives respectively:

- To implement a tight monetary and fiscal policy,
- To reduce inflation,
- To enhance momentum of development by activating idle capacities,
- To liberalize foreign trade, encourage foreign capital investments,
- To take required precautions for establishing interest and exchange rates in (liberal) competitive market.
- To prevent interruption on prices,
- To reduce and stabilize real wages
- To liberalize importation.

These goals are mainly oriented towards restricting state's activity and reducing public intervention in economy. The first legal regulation about privatization in Turkey was made through February 29th 1984 dated and 2983 numbered legislation, which also established the corporate mechanism of privatization. In subsequent periods a number of arrangements were made to obviate the difficulties encountered in the realization of privatization objectives. As a result of these efforts, the principles, strategies, procedures, authorised agencies and problems regarding privatization are all set out in the Privatization Law No. 4046, dated November 27th 1994. Despite these legal regulations, a positive and efficient period couldn't be achieved through privatization-oriented discussions and practices starting in 1980's and intensifying by 1990's. Political instability can be considered as an important reason for this problem. There have been 17 governmental (Cabinet) changes since 1980 and this reflects the nature of this political instability.

As it is mentioned above desired goals pertinent to privatization practices couldn't be achieved in Turkey for various reasons. As seen in Figure-2 the revenue of the privatization between the period of 1985–1997 is only around $3.6 billion. In recent years the process of privatization has gained momentum with the influence of international financial institutions such as the IMF and the World Bank and privatization revenue for the period 2004–2007 has reached up to $22 billion.

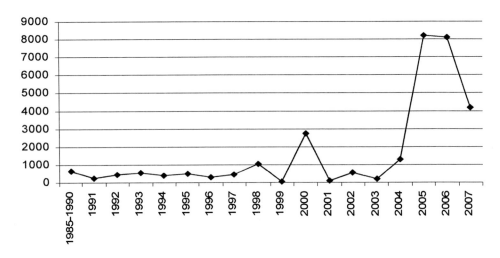

Source: (TPA, 2007).

Figure 2. Privatization Revenues in Turkey, by Region, 1985–2007 ($US millions).

Privatization practices in Turkey between 1985 and 2007 have been implemented in accordance with some methods such as block sale, asset sale, public offering, international offering, I.S.E. (Istanbul Stock Exchange) sale, incompleted asset sale and sales to investment funds. $30 billion revenue of this period has been obtained respectively from block sale %61, public offering %17, asset sale %16, ISE sale %4, and %2 from sales to investment funds respectively (TPA, 2007).

4. A SOE-Privatization Coordinated Regulation Approach: The Second Best Theorem Based Welfare Model

When dealing with global scale competitive power it becomes clear that multinational corporations representing firms and industries are considered as main decision makers; governments, national policy makers are undermined as secondary decision maker units. Thus global economic order lacks social content when compared with national economic order, global income distribution is impaired and Walras's *"ethical efficiency"* concept loses its meaning. We tried to give brief information about the structure of SOEs, which have an important role in the development of countries including Turkey, and evaluate divesting system from public property to private ownership and mention the results of privatization practices. In global scale arguments for increasing competitive power of firms and industries involve micro policies and arguments for increasing national competitive power involve macro policies. Macro references are considered poor as opposed to the micro ones in Krugman and Reinert's competitive power definition. Below, we propose a regulation model which is a combination of the macro and micro policies to synthesize Krugman and Reinert's approaches. The main objective of this chapter is to establish a model that will distinguish the factors that improve the national competitive power. This model, which considers efficiency criteria as a prequisite; aims to realize public life quality and productivity rise simultaneously. Only then, the increase of international trade performance could be accepted as the dynamic for global competitive power and the sufficiency condition of our model may be fulfilled.

4.1. Privatization as a Means for Regulations

Privatization is a competition policy for providing firms of public property with sustainable regulation and competitive power as well as the establishment and enhancement of global competitive environment. It also involves restricting public regulation fields in favor of market and firms. The main point of privatization hypothesis is that public firms will not be able to obtain a sustainable regulation power which will provide them competitive superiority. Therefore SOEs will lack entrepreneurship, creativity, cooperation and adaptability to technological developments and will have structure that can't bear bargaining power. The lack of regulation capability in public enterprises spontaneously limits the regulation fields of cooperating firms and prevents them from using their power optimally or makes it difficult for them to use their power. In this context privatization is very important not only for SOEs but also for other firms to optimize their regulation field and power (Kök and Çoban, 2002).

The importance of privatization changes according to four basic factors when considered from global competitive policies point of view. These are (Türkkan, 2001: 235):

- The bigger the proportionate share of SOEs in economy is, the greater importance of privatization in competitive policies will be.
- The lesser SOEs' autonomy in decision making is and the greater SOEs' dependence on public in profit use and loss compensation is, the greater the importance of privatization in competitive policies will be.
- The more the restriction on the existence of private sectors in SOEs' activity field is, the greater the importance of privatization in competitive policies will be.
- The more appropriate the methods used and the objectives targeted in privatization for improving and enhancement of competitive environment is, the greater the importance of privatization in competitive policies will be.

The importance of privatization as a restructuring strategy and a global competition policy is of higher value for the first three factors above in developing countries such as Turkey. It becomes more important which objectives and methods will enhance the improvement of competitive environment and sustainable regulation and competitive power.

The implementation of regulation mechanism on SOEs has implicit and explicit objectives in accordance with some limitations. These objectives within the framework of regulation mechanism and competition strategies may be listed as below (Joskow, 1998: 206):

- The products and services produced by the monopolies must be supplied to consumers with a lower price by depending on the regulation. In order the mentioned policy to be effective the monopolies must be obviated and the barriers to market entry must be reduced (The rent extraction goal).
- The regulation mechanism must increase the quality of SOEs' goods and services (The supply-side efficiency goal).
- The regulation must increase the attractiveness of SOEs' goods and services through consumer's eyes and the structure and level of prices for the services and goods must be lowered as compared with private sector (The demand-side efficiency goal).
- The investors must be provided with more appropriate conditions in accordance with the regulations and thus investments should be made more attractive. By this way not only will the existence of capital stock be maintained but also additional capital will be provided to sectors. This regulation procedure both increases the revenues of investments and reduces capital costs of firms (The capital attraction or firm viability goal).
- The regulation mechanism arranges income redistribution and ensures that general taxation and spending policies are implemented efficiently by regulating price pattern and price level for SOEs (The income redistribution goal).

It's of crucial importance that regulation mechanism for national competition should be managed effectively in order to achieve the above mentioned goals. The difficulties and delays encountered in the process of privatization which is considered to be a strategy to enhance resource allocation efficiency and competitive power, show that it will be difficult to restrict public's regulation field in favor of market and firms. For this reason it will be fruitful if acquired and practiced experiences are exploited in the privatization policies aiming to restrict the public's own regulation field. The developments happening in Turkey show that public won't be eager to restrict its own regulation and activity sphere without a serious internal and external pressure.

Briefly, in Turkey where privatization practices are turned into a deadlock, the decisions and plans pertinent to public goods have been transformed into bureaucratic choice because of unstable democratic structure which restricts the participation of social groups. Therefore, bureaucracy is the institutional reason for undermining effective competition and productivity phenomena by obtaining an attractive and special position in decisions and plans pertinent to public goods. Inefficiency in resource allocation increases instability thus giving rise to misconducts in employment and government job sharing and as a result *"bad administration in mismanaged democracies drives out good managements"*. If we think that economy policy regulations are themselves public good because of the emerging vicious circle, the importance of creating a competitive regulation model for public goods will increase (Kök, 1995: 173–175). A theoretical framework for the development of a regulation model will be outlined in the next section acting from the case of Turkey to the attention of developing countries.

4.2. A Welfare Model Based on the Second Best Theory: Eco-democratic Contract Approach

The main objective of economic theory is to analyze the harmony mechanism based on safety and production-division which explains how a "satisfactory welfare level" will be achieved with limited possibilities. The concept of harmony, which forms the core point of Eco-Democratic Contract analysis, stands for the collaboration between individuals' benefits and the basic requirements of society and the state which represents the society. Here the dynamic efficiency scale is taken as a reference point. The economic decision units, who are the real owners of national resources, should believe that there exists a safety based model for distribution and should have the power to test this belief in accordance with the political process as they are the representatives of the decision making authority. This will enable the benefit of factor endowments and production to be analyzed with a sustainable equilibrium. In this context, A Regulation Approach Based on SOE-Privatization Cooperation may be developed in accordance with the basic function of SOEs to generate net social benefit and the main objective of private enterprises to obtain maximum profit. According to this approach;

Private Enterprises' Objective Function:

$$\text{Max. Profit} = \text{Total Revenue} - \text{Total Cost}$$

SOEs' Objective Function:

$$\text{Max. Net Social Benefit} = \text{Total Revenue} - \text{Total Cost} \pm \text{Externalities} + \text{Consumer Surplus}$$

It will be beneficial to focus primarily on the scope of ±externalities and to briefly discuss this concept. "Externality is known as positive or negative impact of an economic agent (an individual or a firm) on another agent's production, revenue, free time, assets or welfare". A.C. Pigou has been the first economist to focus systematically on externalities in 1912. According to Pigou, considering negative externalities, Pareto-type (Type I) welfare cannot be maximized even in perfect competition markets. Let's think of an economy with two consumers and two commodities in which the efficiency requisite in exchange is fulfilled. According to this, effective allocation may be explained as a position in which no individual can be made better off without another being made worse off. This may be considered for a situation in which the products are reallocated among the individuals upon conclusion of a trade having advantages for both sides.

As long as externalities aren't taken into account and each individuals' satisfaction are up to his own choice each competitive equilibrium such as hypothetically described W0,W1,... Wm and detailed in the below Figure-3 are accepted as a Pareto optimal allocation process. In this restricted figurative economy, if the income distribution among the consumers were worsened (actual circumstances) and if the government were to intervene (in accordance with eco-democratic contract approach) in initial hardware to enhance a fair income distribution; the market would reach an equilibrium (for example in graphic W'2 with a minimizable deviation) itself in a point far from the competitive equilibrium points. This situation is described as the "second theorem of welfare economics" (Ruffin, 1992).

Imagine that this intervention is performed in a way to have an impact on supply-side factor endowment in economy. Therefore, it is possible to divert supply-side resources from private sector to public sectors or vice versa. In 1960's Ronald Coase pointed to the importance of having a retrospective outlook on history claiming that administration costs would exceed the revenue of eliminating economical inefficiency while, on the other hand, implied consent on Pigou's thesis, who said social welfare would be improved as a result of state's effective policies. If Coase's approach could be turned into a competitive regulation model; that's to say if the state basically removes uncertainty from competition by endorsing its property rights about the production of special welfare goods to private sector, efficiency might be achieved by minimizing state intervention and negative externality disorder might be resolved. For example, when there is a negative externality, optimal condition may be achieved by laying an appropriate tax on the production factor creating negativity or on the final product or an employment policy which resets populism in recruiting human resources may be lawfully legalized. The amount of tax laid must be minimally proportional to monetary value (social cost) negative externality. The employment policy must be transformed into a norm maximizing technical progress. In addition, positive externalities are perceived as a phenomenon which targets net social benefit since their revenues are in the form of subvention.

Because SOEs' main goal in trying to maximize net social benefit (NSB) also increases the operatability of economic models which take Pareto's the second best theorem as reference point. The four basic objectives which entail the emergence of SOEs and which reflect political, social and economical aspects may be achieved if the objective function appropriate to the essence of SOEs and the imperfect competition provisory and gradually monopolizing objective function of competitive private sectors are observed together and handled in a way that covers NSB>SOE Profit<Monopolistic Profit constraint. By this way, it may also be possible to prevent the failure of market mechanism which operates with a SOE-Privatization Combined Regulation Approach, enhance stability, divert the structure of income distribution towards large public communities. Consequently, a constitutional process, which is based on the main principles and which is established through the participatory collaboration of individuals who make decision, may be initiated.

The Second Best Theorem Based Welfare Model may be remodeled as a general model for developing economies based on the case of Turkey and may be listed under the following headings when discussed as an Eco-Democratic Contract Approach. These are to:

- Eliminate the privileges of some sections of the society,
- Minimize unfair competition and establish fair competition conditions,
- Pay special attention to stability and productivity based distribution by the state,
- Prevent voluntary and populist resource allocation by the state when fulfilling its main functions, in other words activating productive resource allocation.

In order for the state to develop a regulation model in accordance with the above mentioned factors, a social benefit-cost analysis must be performed through a *"National Performance Assessment Centre"*. This necessity may be explained with the Walras (1860) principal. The need to evaluate liberalism, which increases production and welfare, and evidences of socialist doctrine, which analysis the direction of improving welfare, and to generate new approaches from that evaluation still remains important. Therefore economists must attach importance to *"human efficiency"*, which is based on the combination of *"scientific efficiency"* and *"ethical efficiency"* (Kök, 1999: 209).

A new regulation model is suggested below considering the above mentioned apprehensions and the privatization goals, economical, social, political motivations and methods of privatization which are already known in the literature. The difficulties encountered in decision making and coordination structure pertinent to public goods and various circumstances whose functional operatability is discussed in Turkish economic system. For example, while planning and decision making process of public good is generally maintained in accordance with the structure of the state, political system and legal regulations, this is not true for Turkey. The main reason for this is the inefficient or lacking regulations in corporeal content and actual practices of the current parliamentary system, which does not play any real role in regulating or monitoring the SOEs. This prevents the occurrence of free and flexible demands for public goods. On the other hand, the production, decision and preferences in relation with public goods are not only specified in accordance with political and administrative decisions but also far from the principle of rationality. There seems to be arbitrariness in political and administrative decision making processes in Turkey because the quality of rational and planned behavior is not well settled off in the minds of people. The principle of rationality in decision making and planning processes of public goods must be observed particularly in the commitments made during the political elections and alternative preferences policy must be put to vote and implemented. In current economic order an ineffective system of production and distribution of public goods is dominant. Such a system may be seen more in developing countries for this reason. The supporters of global competition use this as an argument on privatization.

Basic Assumptions of Model and Dynamic Efficiency:

The five basic assumptions for the analysis of dynamic efficiency in the model are:

1. Political liberalism and power doctrine experiences resulting from it are inefficient in fulfilling promised satisfactory welfare level.

2. Economies of scope resulting from global competition realize monopolizing process.

3. Human as an economic decision unit is not only homoeconomicus, but also homosociologicus in his decisions on supply and demand.

4. Public and private welfare goods both complement and substitute for each other in supply, production and marketing processes.

5. Economical efficiency, which is the major dynamic of welfare economy, is a basic scale for the Second Best Theorem Based Eco-Democratic Contract, which the reference point of resource allocation. This scale is used as a reference indicator for the proper implementation of the model by *"Performance Assessment Centre"* of each country.

In accordance with the above mentioned assumptions it is necessary to define the mechanism of The Second Best Based Welfare Model embodying the SOE-Privatization Combination.

The concept of "Dynamic Efficiency" may be manifested in Cartesian frame in the following way: Let's suppose that general efficiency level of economic decision units may be determined within specific periods (year, 20 years) and let's associate a country's production structure with the production function of a multi-product firm or industry (agriculture, automotive, rubber industry etc.); as it is shown in Figure-3, let's think that private welfare goods producer A ($A_{(K,L)}^{X\,\mathrm{Pr}\,W}$) produced an X private welfare goods in private sector, B

($B_{(K,L)}^{YPW}$) produced a Y public welfare goods and put these on axes of coordinate system.

According to this, a nation, has the capital and labour stock by which it can produce both

$$\sum_{i=1}^{m} X1, X2....Xm = \sum_{i=1}^{m} X \; ; \text{and} \sum_{i=1}^{m} Y1, Y2....Ym = \sum_{i=1}^{m} Y \text{ goods in the length of coordinate}$$

axes. Let's give W0 to the equilibrium on the *"Eco-Democratic Contract Curve"* in accordance with Pareto's first welfare theorem (fundamental theorems of welfare economics) and data production factors shown in Figure-3 (W0, W1.....Wm equilibrium hypothesis in hypothetical exchange). According to this, the welfare level corresponding to any point in Cartesian coordinate system will display each of WP and WPr goods combination which can be produced using a nation's capital stock. For example M0, M2, M4, M6, M10 refer to indifference curves group, WP refers to origin convex curves; and m1, m3, m5, m7, m9 indifference curves refer to convex curves to WPr origin.

According to *Orthodox Standard Economic Theory*, indifference curves under perfect competition conditions, $MRTS_{(K,L)}^{X\,\mathrm{Pr}\,W} = MRTS_{(K,L)}^{YPW} = \frac{P_L}{P_K}$ is fulfilled when it's equilibrium on welfare transformation curve (Eco–Democratic Contract Curves) is seen. The condition in which producer equilibrium and consumer (A, B) equilibrium ($MRS_{(X,Y)}^{X\,\mathrm{Pr}\,W} = MRS_{(X,Y)}^{YPW} = \frac{P_y}{P_x}$) is fulfilled correspondingly $\left(MRTS_{(K,L)}^{X\,\mathrm{Pr}\,W} = MRTS_{(K,L)}^{YPW} \right) = \left(MRS_{(X,Y)}^{X\,\mathrm{Pr}\,W} = MRS_{(X,Y)}^{YPW} \right)$ is known as the Micro General Equilibrium. In fact, the hypothetical equilibrium, which is a combination of production function emerging within the framework of econometric model, is not W_0, it may be $W_0^{'}$ (error term: ε is included in the model). If we turn back to above named model; The Welfare Model based on The Second Best Theorem which is predicated on the idea that SOE and private sector factor endowments is reallocated in accordance with privatization process; may be explained with accessible potential equilibrium $W_3^{'}$ according to Eco-Democratic Contract Approach. The model shown here, is the discussion about to what extent it would be possible to privatize the capital accumulation connected with SOE in order for the public to reach "satisfactory welfare" level. When the analysis pertinent to Pareto Type I ideal equilibrium shown in Figure-3 as W_0 (W_1.....W_m) (The first theorem of welfare economics) and Pareto Type II deviated economic equilibrium shown as $W_3^{'}$, which is handled from the econometric point of view, (second theorem of welfare economics) are considered together we can reach to $W_3^{'}$ with a regulation modeling from the W_0 equilibrium point, which emerged with a dynamic efficiency scale at first. Here the main expectation is not only the verification of the second best theorem, but also the minimization of inefficiency in $W_3^{'}$ equilibrium process which is accepted as empirical equilibrium point as a substitute for hypothetic efficiency. Thus, the Eco-Democratic Contract Approach pertinent to production, division or consumption of private and public welfare goods accepts that the real equilibrium is within the band region specified by dynamic process. One of the main reasons of this inefficiency is the inability to control some of the variables which cause externality. Hypothetical equilibrium process of the standard theory cannot be interrogated since these ambiguities, which can be explained mainly with information economies and land rents, aren't included in the model. However, this ambiguities vector may be included in the model in compliance with developments in mathematical statistics. The second reason is the political choices which cause wrong resource allocations (Privatization rationality). For that reason the models which don't include externalities in public production area and internalities in the private production area aren't applicable. In this context, A Regulation Approach representing SOE-Privatization Combination which combines the above mentioned satisfactory welfare model of production and net social benefit function eliminates the instability generated by the concept of global scale monopolizing and this necessitates that the goal function is redefined (Kök, 1995: 175).

Another main objective of the model is to state that it is impossible for the nations to neglect division-safety component. Therefore, the rationale for intervention to privatization may sometimes conflict or overlap with the rationale for intervention to nationalization. In this context, this paradox must be resolved in the dynamic equilibrium process. In this case, a model based on satisfactory welfare rather than welfare maximization as introduced in Traditional Economy Theory must be established. Here privatization procedure must transform capital accumulation model into efficiency production model correspondingly with basic phases of general socio-economic development process. For this reason it is of paramount importance that a model based on production, division and safety is developed because the monopolistic structure, a probable consequence of pure efficiency hypothesis, may threaten the social reconciliation. The greatest advantage of this model is that it places the dynamic efficiency at the focal point of welfare transfer mechanism (Kök, 1995: 131).

Therefore, it will be necessary to minimize the gap between "actual equilibrium" (including all positive and negative deviations) and "ideal equilibrium" targeted in perfect competition and welfare maximization. This equilibrium must be in such an acceptable level that; the welfare level achieved by both private welfare goods (WPr), and public welfare goods (WP) may be simultaneously defined. This analytic approach, may be verified both with mathematical statistics method and "satisfactory welfare combination" (eco-democratic contract approach) which exist in coordinate plane.

In short, "satisfactory welfare" level of both group of goods (such as W0, W0'; W1, W1'; W2, W2'; W3, W3'; W4, W4') will rise proportional to the level of increase in their general efficiency level in the dimensions of time, place and factor. According to this approach, which is explained with simple arithmetical notations, the welfare resulting from production of private-welfare goods and the welfare created by production of public-welfare goods may be shown on Eco-Democratic Contract Curve.

Goal Function:

$$\text{WTE} = [\sum_{i=1}^{m} X1, X2....Xm = \text{Wpr}\sum_{i=1}^{m} X] + [\text{Wp}\sum_{i=1}^{m} Y1, Y2....Ym = \sum_{i=1}^{m} Y]$$

$$\text{WTE} = \alpha 1 + \beta 1 \text{XPr1} + \beta 2 \text{XPr2} + \beta 3 \text{XPr3} + ... + \beta m \text{XPrm} + \alpha 2$$
$$+ \gamma 1 \text{XP1} + \gamma 2 \text{XP2} + \gamma 3 \text{XP3} + ... + \gamma m \text{XPm} + \text{Ut}$$

In the above equation;
WTE: Expected satisfactory total welfare,

WPr: Welfare of private welfare goods production,

WP: Welfare of public welfare goods production,

Constraint function: XPr1, XPr2, XPr3, ..., XPrm: Private welfare goods and factor endowment generated by accumulative capital stock in the dimension of time and other production factors;

XP1, XP2, XP3, ..., XPm: Public welfare goods generated by accumulative capital stock in the dimension of time and other production factors,

$\beta 1$, $\beta 2$, $\beta 3$, ...,βm: Input flexibilities obtained from private welfare goods production function,

$\gamma 1$, $\gamma 2$, $\gamma 3$, ...,γm: Input flexibilities obtained from public welfare goods production function,

$\alpha 1$: Technical efficiency parameter of production function to private welfare goods,

$\alpha 2$: Technical efficiency parameter of production function to public welfare goods,

Ut: error term added to production function of each industry

According to this, WTE = WPr+WP "satisfactory welfare combinations" may be specified in Eco-Democratic Contract Curve. In fact this equilibrium is similar with the general equilibrium in micro economic theory.

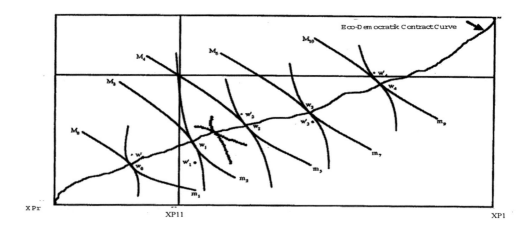

Figure 3. Eco-Democratic Contract and Factor Endowment Efficiency.

As shown in Figure-3, individual welfare and national competition is related with sustainable production of both private and public goods and factor income sharing. The general equilibrium, which simultaneously maintains production and consumption efficiency of both private and public goods, may be defined with the success of a Regulation Approach with SOE-Privatization Combination which is established in accordance with political choices.

5. Result and Suggestions

There is a need to establish new models in order to achieve efficient resources allocation and fair income division in developing countries in the global competition process. The handling of SOEs' with an Eco-Democratic Contract Model as it is suggested in this chapter may establish a guideline for the prevention of results of a pure free economy leading a wild capitalism and of transformation of certain challanges to certain opportinuties.

Uneasiness of citizens in developing countries' may be retrenched with such an approach. Likewise, the anxiety formed by inward-oriented national economy policies may be avoided. By this model it will be possible to avoid public doubt about foreign capital and block foreign capital's aim of transnational hegemony formation. On the other hand, it will be crucial for the right questioning of utopical tendency of few multinational firms to establish a single world state, which is "policeman of the world".

Economists' search for such economic models may enhance scientific search programs because they will enable them to explain new global conditions with new paradigms. Because the main economic model for the states representing power is not the model which describes how global factor endowments have been monopolized. These are the models which describe the ways by which the inequality/poorness resulting from the allocation of limited global resources in a unipolar capitalism process can be prevented. It is clear that there is a necessity for such models. We can say that it is urgent that long-term renewable production and consumption circulation is maintained and even an Eco-Democratic Contract system, covering man and social reconciliation, is established.

In conclusion, the main goal of Eco-Democratic Contract model, which is established for empowering national industry, is to explain the dynamics for achieving global competition power on condition that national competition power is maintained. If this model is put into practice, it will be possible to overcome the artificial difficulties encountered in some stages of national development process, to internalize information economies, to develop a method of persuasion enabling us to use domestic savings to overcome capital insufficiency and to create a dynamic force which will enable national economy to take place in global competition, as well.

Acknowledgement

We thank our colleagues Şevki Özgener, Gürhan Kök, Ali Ulusoy, Can Tansel Tugcu and Neşe Yalçın Seçme who reviewed the manuscript.

References

Bai, C., Li, D. D. & Wang, Y. (1997). Enterprise productivity and efficiency: When is up really down?. *Journal of Comparative Economics*, **24** (3), 265-280.

Banterle, A. (2005). Competitiveness and agri-food trade: An empirical analysis in the Europen Union. In S. Rasmussen (Eds.), *The future of rural Europe in the global agri-food system (pp. 1-13),* Paper presented at the 11th Congress of the EAAE. August 24-27. Copenhagen, Denmark.

Barberis, N., Boycko, M., Shleifer, A. & Tsukanova, N. (1996). How does privatization work? Evidence from the Russian shops. *Journal Political Economy*, **104** (4), 764-790.

Begg, I. (2002). Urban competitiveness: policies for dynamic cities, Bristol: The Policy Press.

Boardman, A. & Vining, A. R. (1989). Ownership and performance in competitive environments: A comparison of the performance of private, mixed, and state-owned enterprises. *Journal Law Economics, 32,* 1-33.

Boubakri, N. & Cosset J. C. (2002). Does privatization meet the expectations? Evidence from african countries. *Journal of African Economies,* 111-140.

Boubakri, N. & Cosset, J. (1998). The financial and operating performance of newly privatized firms: evidence from developing countries. *The Journal of Finance,* 1083-1112.

Boubakri, N., Cosset, J. C. & Guedhami, O. (2005). Liberalization, corporate governance and the performance of newly privatized firms. *Journal of Corporate Finance, 11,* 767-790.

Boycko, M., Shleifer, A. & Vishny, R.W. (1996). A theory of privatization. *Economic Journal,* **106** (435), 309–319.

Budd, L. & Hirmis, A (2004). Conceptual framework for regional competitiveness. *Regional Studies,* **38** (9), 1015-1028.

Çakal, R. (1996). *Doğal tekellerde özelleştirme ve regülasyon,* Ankara: DPT Yayını No. 2455.

Çoban, O. & Seçme, G. (2005). Prediction of socio-economical consequences of privatization at the firm level with fuzzy cognitive mapping, *Information Sciences,* **169** (1-2), 131-154.

Cockburn, J., Siggel, E., Coulibaly, M. & Vézina, S. (1999). Measuring competitiveness and its sources: The case of Mali's manufacturing sector. *Canadian Journal of Development Studies,* **20** (3), 491-519.

Cremer, H., Marchand, M. & Thisse, J. F. (1989). The public firm as an instrument for regulating an oligopolistic market. *Oxford Economic Papers,* **41,** 283–301.

D'Souza, J. & Megginson, W. (1999). The financial and operating performance of privatized firms during the 1990s. *Journal of Finance, 54,* 1397–1438.

Depperu, D. & Cerrato, D. (2005). *Analyzing international competitiveness at the firm level: concepts and measures. Working Paper* No.. **32,** Dipartimento Scienze Sociali - Sezione Economia Aziendale, Universita Cattolica del Sacro Cuore, Piacenza.

Djankov, S. & Murrell, P. (2000). The determinants of enterprise restructuring in transition: An assessment of the evidence. Washington, D.C.: World Bank.

Djankov, S. & Murrell, P. (2002). Enterprise restructuring in transition: A quantitative survey. *Journal of Economic Literature,* **40** *(3),* 739–792.

Domberger, S. & Piggott, J. (1986). Privatisation policies and public enterprise: A survey. *The Economic Record,* **62** (2), 145-160.

Estache, A. (2001). Privatization and regulation of transport ınfrastructure in the 1990s. *The Worldbank Research Observer,* **16** (1), 85-107.

Ghosh Banerjee, S. & Rondinelli, D. A. (2003). Does foreign aid promote privatization? Empirical evidence from developing countries. *World Development,* **31**(9), 1527–1548.

Haataja, M. & Okkonen, J. (2005). *Competitiveness of knowledge intensive services.* eBRF eBusiness Research Forum Conference, Tampere, August 20-22, 2004.

Harper, J. T. (2002). The performance of privatized firms in the Czech Republic. *Journal of Banking and Finance,* **26** (4), 621-649.

Havrylyshyn, O., & McGettigan, D. (1999). *Privatization in transition countries: A sampling of the literature. IMF, Working Paper* No. **99/6.**

Hayek, F. A. (1978). The confusion of language in political thought. In F.A. Hayek (Eds.), *New studies in philosophy, politics, economics and the history of ideas* (pp. 71–97). London: Routledge & Kegan Paul.

Henricsson, J.P.E, Ericsson, S., Flanagan, R. & Jewell, C.A. (2004). Rethinking competitiveness for the construction industry. In F. Khosrowshahi (Eds.). *Proceedings 20th Annual ARCOM Conference* (Vol 1, 9pp), Heriot-Watt University, Edinburgh, September.

Jones, S. L., Megginson, W. L., Nash, R. C. & Netter, J. M.. (1999). Share issue privatizations as financial means to political and economic ends. *Journal of Finance Economics*, **53**, 217-253.

Joskow, P. L. (1998). *Regulatory priorities for reforming infrastructure sectors in developing countries. The 10th Annual Bank Conference on Development Economics*, April 20-21, Washington, D.C.: World Bank.

Kitson, M. Martin, R. & Tyler, P. (2004). Regional competitiveness: An elusive yet key concept? *Regional Studies*, **38**(9), 991-999.

Kök, R. & Çoban, O. (2002). Kitlere ilişkin bir regülasyon modelinin gerekliliği ve kaynak kullanım etkinliği üzerine: Nevşehir tekel rakı fabrikası örneği, *6th METU International Conference in Economics*, Ankara: September 11-14, (2002), (publishing in CD-ROM). Available at: http://www.econ.utah.edu/ehrbar/erc2002/abstracts/A180.html.

Kök, R. (1995). Ekonomi-politik, popülizm: Özelleştirme ve KİT'ler, İstanbul: Dergah Yayınları.

Kök, R. (1999). *İktisadi düşünce: Kavramların analitik evrimi*, İzmir: Anadolu Matbaacılık.

Kole, S. R. & Mulherin, J. H. (1997). The government as a shareholder: A case from the United States. *Journal of Law & Economics*, **40**(1), 1-22.

Krugman, P. (1994). Competitiveness: a dangerous obsession. *Foreign Affairs*, **73** (2), 28-44.

La Porta, R. & López-de-Silanes, F. (1999). Benefits of privatization evidence from Mexico. *Quarterly Journal of Economics*, **114**, 1193-1242.

Laffont, J. J. & Tirole, J. (1993). *A Theory of incentives in procurement and regulation.* Cambridge, MA: MIT Press.

Lin, C. (2000). *Corporate governance of state-owned enterprises in China.* Working Paper, Manila: Asian Development Bank.

Lin, J. Y., Fang, C. & Li, Z. (1998). Competition, policy burdens, and state-owned enterprise reform. *The American Economic Review*, **88** (2), 422-427.

Lizal, L., Singer, M. & Svejnar, J. (2001). Enterprise breakups and performance during the transition from plan to market. *Review of Economics and Statistics*, **83**(1), 92-99.

Marchand, M., Pestieau, P. & Tulkens, H. (1984). The performance of public enterprises: normative, positive and empirical issues. In M. Marchand, P. Pestieau & H. Tulkens (Eds.). *The performance of public entreprises: concepts and measurement* (pp. 3-42), Amsterdam: North-Holland.

Megginson, W. & Netter, J. (2001). From state to market: A survey of empirical studies on privatization. *Journal of Economic Literature*, **39**, 321–389.

Megginson, W., Nash, R. & Randenborgh, M. (1994). The financial and operating performance of newly privatized firms: An international empirical analysis. *Journal of Finance*, **49**, 403–452.

Megginson, W., Nash, R., Netter, J. & Poulsen, A. (2004). The choice of private versus public capital markets: Evidence from privatizations. *Journal of Finance,* **59,** 2835–2870.

Nellis, J. (1999). *Time to rethink privatization in transition economies? IFC Discussion Paper* No. **38,** Washington, D.C.: World Bank Group.

Nellis, J. (2000). *Privatization in transition economies: What next? Working Paper,* Washington D.C.: World Bank.

TPA (Republic Of Turkey Prime Ministry Privatization Administration). (2007), http://www.oib.gov.tr/program/implementations.htm

Perelman, S. & Pestieau, P. (1988). Technical performance in public enterprises: A comparative study of railways and postal services. *European Economic Review,* **32,** 432–441.

Porter, M. E. (1990). *The competitive advantage of nations.* Londra, Basingstoke: Macmillan.

Price Waterhouse. (1989a). Privatization: Learning the lessons from the U.K. experience, London: Price Waterhouse.

Price Waterhouse, (1989b). *Privatization: The facts,* London: Price Waterhouse.

Privatization. (2007). *Privatization trends and statistics.* Available at: http://www.privatization.org/database/trendsandstatistics.html.

Ramamurti, R. (1987). Leadership styles in state-owned enterprises, *Journal of General Management,* **13** (2), 45-55.

Ramanathan, R. (1986). *A Note on the Lagrange multiplier test and model selection criteria.* University of California San Diego *Discussion Paper* No. **86-19.**

Reinert, E. (1994). Catching-up from way behind. A third world perspective on first world history. In J. Fagerberg and others (Eds.), *The dynamics of technology, trade and growth* (pp. 283-301), Aldershot, U.K.: Edward Elgar Publishing.

Ruffin, R.J. (1992). *Intermediate microeconomics.* Fourth Edition, New York: Harper Collins.

Saygılı, Ş. & Taymaz, E. (1996). Türkiye çimento sanayinde özelleştirme ve teknik etkinlik. *ODTÜ Gelişme Dergisi,* **23** (3), 405-426.

Sheshinski, E. & Lopez-Calva, L. F. (2003). Privatization and its benefits: theory and evidence, *CESifo Economic Studies,* **49** (3), 429–459

Shirley, M. & Walsh, P. (2000). *Public vs. private ownership: the current state of the debate.* World Bank Policy Research Working Paper No. 2420, Washington, D.C.: The World Bank.

Shleifer, A. (1998). State versus private ownership. *Journal of Economic Perspectives,* **12** (4), 133-150.

Siggel, E. & Cockburn, J., (1995). *International competitiveness and its sources: a method of development policy analysis.* Concordia University, Department of Economics, *Discussion Paper* No. **9517.**

Türkkan, E. (2001). *Rekabet teorisi ve endüstri iktisadı,* Ankara: Turhan Kitabevi.

Vickers, J. & Yarrow, G. (1991). Economic perspectives on privatization. *Journal of Economic Perspectives,* **5,** 111-132.

Vining, A. R. & Boardman, A. (1992). Ownership versus competition: Efficiency in public enterprise. *Public Choice,* **73,** 205-239.

World Bank. (2002). *Global development finance.* Washington, DC: Worldbank.

World Bank. (2007). *Privatization database.* Available at: http://rru.worldbank.org/ Privatization/Region.aspx?regionid=999.

Yergin, D. & Stanislaw, J. (1998). The commanding heights: the battle between government and the marketplacethat is remaking the modern world, New York: Simon & Schuster

Zeckhauser, R.J. & Horn, M. (1989). The control and performance of state-owned enterprises. In MacAvoy, P.W., Stanbury, W. T., Yarrow, G., & Zeckhauser, R. J. (Eds.), *Privatization and state-owned enterprises* (pp. 7-58), Boston: Kluwer.

In: Global Privatization and Its Impact
Editors: I.J. Hagen and T.S. Halvorsen, pp. 87-101
ISBN: 978-1-60456-785-4
© 2008 Nova Science Publishers, Inc.

Chapter 5

GLOBAL PRIVATIZATION IN ENERGY SECTORS: GLOBAL "PRIMITIVE ACCUMULATION"[±]

Serdal Bahçe[*]

Faculty of Political Sciences, Ankara University

" ...[A]s soon as the question of property is at stake, it becomes a sacred duty to proclaim the standpoint of the nursery tale as the one thing fit for all age-groups and all stages of development. In actual history, it is a notorious fact that **conquest, enslavement, robbery,** murder, in short, **force plays the greatest part**"

Marx[1]

"**Force, fraud, oppression, looting** are openly displayed without any attempt at concealment, and it requires an effort to discover within this tangle of political violence and contests of power the stern laws of the economic process"

Rosa Luxemburg[2]

Abstract

The world-wide privatization and liberalization of energy sectors have been one of the contemporary exhibitions of permanent "primitive accumulation" process. Apart from varieties displayed by various countries in their liberalization and privatization experiences, all these experiences have displayed some common characteristics: privatization by force, blackmail, fraud and corruption. These common characteristics have been central to the so-called "primitive accumulation" process. This process, inherently, has ended up losers (reforming countries, governments, households...etc.) and also winners (international energy firms, privatization consultancy firms, capital as whole...etc.).

[±] The author is grateful to Dr. Seçil A. Kaya-Bahçe for her helpful comments. The author is also thankful to Public Services International Research Unit for allowing him to benefit from their database.
[*] E-mail address: sbahce@politics.ankara.edu.tr
[1] Marx, 1990: 874.
[2] Quoted by De Angelis, 2006.

I. Introduction

The maelstrom of liberalism have been spreading the whole globe with the aid of addicted bureaucrats, well-armed institutions and eager scholars. The basic motto behind this thundering project is "private property ensures efficiency and lower costs" and this motto, in line with neo-liberal creed, wandered around the world and infiltrate into every national economic agenda. This contagious movement have unceasingly leaped from one sector to another and commons and public utility sectors have fallen into the range of neo-liberal bullets one by one. Finally, "Hayekian counter-revolution"[3] extended its boundaries beyond the energy sectors.

In the context of sectors in the privatization range, this contagious movement- since its genesis- has been continuously asserting that publicly owned sectors and enterprises have proved to be poor performers in terms of efficiency and financial statements (Kessides, 2005: 82). Especially in energy sectors, new technological developments have undermined the so-called "natural monopoly" situation; i.e. new technological opportunities nullify the basic premises of the case for natural monopolies (Newberry, 1997).[4] Moreover, new public economics excommunicates the idea that public provision of energy is a right of every citizen and also a responsibility for governments.[5] The radical transformation of economic rhetoric coincided with the global accumulation crisis which signaled itself in the end of the 1960s, but culminated in the 1970s and 1980s. This crisis paved the way for a quest for new highly profitable areas of internationalized capital and, hence, the state-owned or strictly regulated public utilities offered new profitable opportunities. Moreover, the appropriation of public utility sectors, coupled with new legal and institutional arrangements, also serves to reduce the circulating capital costs.[6] The abolition of cross subsidies which were generally designed to ensure the partial finance of the consumption of low-income groups by high-income groups and reduction in tax rates on energy reduces the costs of circulating capital. Unbundling of energy sectors have opened new investment areas and highly specialized companies flocked into artificially-created new sectors which emerged just after unbundling. Moreover, these new profitable areas have brought about new professions; as a result, new finance project and consultant firms have swarmed over energy sectors. Therefore, energy sector privatizations have proved to be very effective in curing the problems occurred as a result of over-accumulation of capital.

Privatization of energy sectors has been a global phenomenon which quickly transgressed the national boundaries. Therefore, any assessment of the results of and analysis of privatization should be handled in international context. As international financial institutions

---

[3]Watts, 2006:5.

[4]Yi-chong briefly analyzed the radical break through in economic thinking about electricity sectors (Yi-chong,1005).

[5] For the case of electricity, Rochlin overtly denounces the common belief that electricity is a right: "Electricity need not to be a right. If consumers face the volatility inherent in wholesale prices, the obligation to serve is no longer the sole domain of third parties and barriers to entry are minimized, then electricity can be treated as a commodity. However, if electricity continues to be treated as a right, at least consumers and politicians should know that it does involve significant (stranded) costs in both generation and transmission" (Rochlin, 2002: 35-36).

[6] Especially after the liberalization of electricity sectors, as large consumers, firms have gained a considerable bargaining power and new market structures and their operating principles have legitimized this power. This is the most important factor that is lying behind the widening of the scissor between the prices paid by industry and trade, and prices paid by households.

have proposed nearly the same program to every capitalist country, it becomes clear that we should conduct such an analysis at international level. In addition to this, the key players in this game, except from "reformer" countries, have become extensively internationalized. International financial institutions have increased the number of contacts to an unprecedented level and internationalized companies, the major beneficiaries from energy sector reforms, have expanded their operations to a huge set of countries. Internationalization, from the perspective of companies, is a way of evasion from regional risks; by this way, they gain considerable flexibility in investment decisions. This flexibilization can also be used for blackmailing the "reformer" countries. In this context, the privatization of energy sectors engraves the epithet of "global".

This study aims to debunk the role of privatization in energy sectors in the contemporary organization of extended capital accumulation. Generally, we agree with the hypothesis that hitherto privatization is modern self-manifestation of the permanent "primitive accumulation". As Section II will implicitly argue, energy resources and assets are conceived to be commons and privatization, in this context, is the direct way of plunder of these commons by private firms and international capital. However, such a pretentious argument should be testified by facts and tendencies. The subsequent section will try to find out the absolute and relative size of privatization in the energy sectors. Then, the third section tries to analyze the international pressures against will-to-privatize countries. These pressures have been analyzed in the context of primitive accumulation hypothesis. The results of these pressures manifest themselves in conditionalities of international financial institutions, the unjust claims of internationalized companies, the pressures of consultancy firms, undervaluation of assets of privatized firms, corruption and oligopolization of energy sectors.

II. Primitive Accumulation: Continious Form of Accumulation by Disposession

For Marx, "primitive accumulation", was a vital phase in the history of capitalism. As an attribute, "primitive" indicates the use of non-economic force in plunder of commons.

> "So-called primitive accumulation , therefore, is nothing else than the historical process of divorcing the producer from the means of production. It appears as 'primitive' because it forms the prehistory of capital, and of the mode of the production corresponding to capital.........In the history of primitive accumulation, all revolutions are epoch making that act as levers for the capitalist class in course of its formation; but this is true above all for those moments when great masses of men are suddenly and forcibly torn from their means of subsistence and hurled on to the labour–market as free, unprotected and rightless proletarians." (Marx, 1990:874-876).

As Marx pointed out above, primitive accumulation serves two basic purposes: to give initial spurt to capital accumulation "to set capital free" and to unbound the bounded labour. Marx, in his magnum opus, started with the analysis of simple commodity and then advanced into the detailed analysis of capital; i.e. capital in the form of living labour and capital in the form of dead labour. However, as a consequence of his dialectical/analytical framework, he did not pay so much attention to the concept of "property" and the evolution of capitalist property. Nevertheless, the chapter on "Primitive Accumulation" in Capital I provides an invaluable insight upon the capital accumulation and property accumulation.

The question whether the process of "primitive accumulation" was a temporary/transitory phase of capitalism or a permanent process operating continuously is the core of a historical debate about the characteristics of capitalism as a historical/social system. The majority of Marxist scholars have been in favor of the former explanation. Even Marx himself explicitly indicated that this process was the initial phase of capitalism.[7] On this side, we can count Lenin, Andre Gunder Frank and a very long list of Marxist scholars. On the other hand, some prominent figures like Rosa Luxembourg and some contemporary scholars like Michael Perelman followed the latter explanation, that is, they have taken primitive accumulation as a continuous process.[8] As the following quotation shows, Rosa Luxemburg believed that "primitive accumulation" was not an archaic tool for capital accumulation, it is a "permanent weapon" which is to be used continuously:

> "Accumulation, with its spasmodic expansion, can no more wait for, and be content with, a natural internal disintegration of non-capitalist formations and their transition to commodity economy, than it can wait for, and be content with, the natural increase of the working population. Force is the only solution open to capital; the accumulation of capital, seen as an historical process, employs force as a permanent weapon, not only at its genesis, but further on down to the present day"(R.Luxemburg, quoted by Grandia, 2007:16).

The scholars belonging to the second tradition, generally viewed this continuous process as a way of the domination of capitalism over pre-capitalist modes of production (as in the case of Samir Amin, see, De Angelis, 2001). However, as De Angelis stressed, since "primitive accumulation", in Marx's works, has two distinctive characteristics; first it represents a strategy to divorce direct producers from the means of production and second, it may exhibit itself in various ways, it can be depicted as a continuous process (De Angelis, 2001: 12).

The core of the debate whether this process is historical or continuous depends on the conditions in which potential labour power is freed. The accumulation of capital coincides with the accumulation of private property. This process also produces its symmetric movement; the accumulation of dispossessed in capitalist society. Being dispossessed does not only mean the lack of ownership of means of production; it also indicates the commodification of every aspect of social life in which dispossessed individuals are forced to engage in waged labour. The essence of primitive accumulation is to ease the symmetrical accumulation of capital and property on one side and accumulation of individuals ready to labour on the other side through the usage of force, pressure and conquest.

Moreover, this adjustment at the property level does not take place only at social class level, it can be observed also at national and international level. Property adjustment covers the transfer of assets from lower classes to upper classes, from state to private investors and also from sovereign states to international firms. Financial and monetary crises have made this adjustment mandatory. The losers from neoliberal structural adjustment programs, states and lower classes are generally dragged towards serious indebtedness, and this, sooner or

---

[7] Werner Bonefeld indicates that in the original German version of *Capital*, primitive accumulation is referred by 'ursprünglich' which could be translated as 'initial', 'beginning' or 'original' (Bonefeld, 2007: 5).

[8] For this discussion see Moore,2004 and De Angelis, 2001.

later, entails an adjustment at asset level. The transfer of assets from losers to winners, e.g. international capital and big firms, as David Harvey puts, is a form of accumulation by dispossession (Harvey, 2005).

The commodification of every aspect in the surrounding neighborhood encapsulates the contemporary privatization of public services and utilities. As will be analyzed in detail below, this sort of primitive accumulation has significant similarities with the historical phase what Marx called as "primitive accumulation". Although citizens paid for some public services and the goods produced by public utilities in pre-privatization period, the welfare-oriented policies of public utilities and direct and indirect transfers made by these utilities generated a protective belt for especially working class and urban middle classes. Privatization, depriving these social classes from this protective belt, makes them more vulnerable to the abuses of capital. Without such a protective belt, these classes are now more and more eager to work longer hours and to participate in labour process.

Moore identified a third function of "primitive accumulation", in addition to the two functions outlined by Marx, as to allocate members of the society the right to buy their independent means of subsistence (Moore, 2004:90). Privatization of energy sectors generates the opportunity for capital to exploit this "right". If members of the society prefer not to use this right, the only alternative will be starvation to death: "With privatization of necessities today, the imposition of markets forces families to get out of the way and succumb to the dictates of capital or put themselves at severe risk. People deprived of clean water die just as tragically as peasants shot by the game wardens of old." (Perelman, 2007:59-60).

III. The Size of the Privatization Pie

The pioneers of privatization and liberalization of energy sectors were Chile and the United Kingdom and most of the capitalist countries have followed them. The privatization history of energy sectors has witnessed three parallel and interrelated developments. First, the number of will-to-privatize countries have increased since the beginning of the 1980s. Second, the number of internationalized firms aiming to appropriate the privatized energy assets have displayed an increasing trend. Third, as will be discussed below, international financial institutions and international banks began to press upon the financially distressed economies to commit themselves to privatization strategy. Moreover, the collapse of Soviet-type socialism and strict commitment of post-socialist governments to liberalization program widened the scope for international capital which aimed to invade energy sectors, since most of the transition economies are abundant in natural and energy resources. In this context, the size of the privatization pie increased to more than $140 billions from 1990 to 2006. More than 80 non-OECD countries have implemented privatization programs in their energy sectors up to 2006.[9]

As Table 1 shows, for the period 1990-2006, privatization proceeds capture about 44 % of the global private investment in energy sectors. Except for the initial year, its share exceeded 60 % only in two years, 1992 and 1997. We should note that the proceeds from concessions hold a very low portion of total privatization proceeds, i.e. % 10 percent for the

---

[9] See, World Bank's Private Participation in Infrastructure database (ppi.worldbank.org).

whole period. Thus, the main driver in privatization was divestiture or the acquisition of public energy assets by private firms.

Table 1. Share of Global Privatization in Private Investment in Energy Sectors

Year	Privatization Proceeds[a] (US $ mil.)	Total Private Investment (US $ mil.)	Share of Privatization (%)
1990	524	592	88.5
1991	129	992	13.0
1992	6,456	9,534	67.7
1993	2,938	12,413	23.7
1994	4,757	14,464	32.9
1995	7,814	21,775	35.9
1996	11,254	29,404	38.3
1997	29,021	46,072	63.0
1998	15,610	29,321	53.2
1999	8,818	20,896	42.2
2000	9,543	25,451	37.5
2001	7,014	17,158	40.9
2002	10,837	20,162	53.7
2003	5,482	20,982	26.1
2004	7,837	15,125	51.8
2005	5,352	17,796	30.1
2006	8,439	19,479	43.3
Total	141,821	321,616	44.1

Source: The World Bank Private Participation in Infrastructure Database (http://ppi.worldbank.org)
[a] Privatization proceeds cover proceeds from concessions and divestitures.

Up to 1997, energy sectors captured the highest share in total private investment in infrastructure sectors.[10] After 1997, telecommunications sector became the most attractive sector. Towards the end of the period 1990-2006, energy sectors fell to the third place after transportation sectors. However, for the whole period, energy sectors attracted 29.5 % of all private investment while telecom sector absorbed 49.2 %. On the other hand, as Figure 1 shows, privatization proceeds from energy sectors were rising until 1997, then displayed a declining trend. The highest figure in 1997[11] was about $29 billion. For the period 1990-2006, the share of privatization proceeds in total privatization proceeds from infrastructure was about 25 %.

Table 2 shows the weight of privatization proceeds at the regional level. As the table confirms, Latin American and the Caribbean countries took the lead in total private investment in energy sectors. Nearly one third of the private investment went to this region.

---

[10] In this period, throughout the whole amount of privatization proceeds, infrastructure and energy sectors captured 65 %, see Kikeri and Kolo, 2005: 13.
[11] Brazil and China are the top two countries in the ranking according to total proceeds from privatization for the period 1990 and 2006.

As for privatization, the same region had been considerably far ahead from other regions. Total privatization proceeds for the period 1990-2006 was slightly higher than $80 billion, which means that 61.6 % of total private investment in this region preferred to buy public assets or take concessions in energy sectors. In addition to these, this region's share in total privatization proceeds from energy sectors is about 57 %. The region having the highest privatization share was Europe/Central Asia region. East and South Asia, and Pacific regions fell behind due to the fact that countries in those regions have generally promoted greenfield projects.

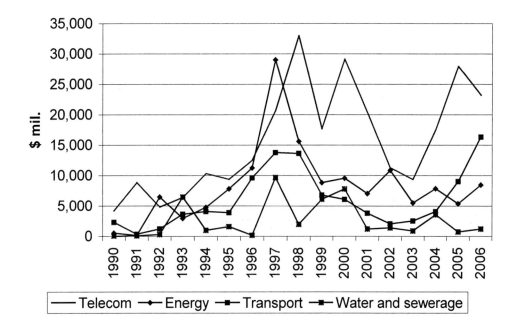

Figure 1. Privatization in Infrastructure Sectors.

Table 2. The Share of Privatization Proceeds in Total Private Investment at a Regional Context, 1990-2006

Region	Privatization Proceeds [a] (US $ mil.)	Total Private Investment (US $ mil.)	Share of Privatization (%)
East Asia and Pacific	18,014	93,753	19.2
Europe and Central Asia	29,410	42,860	68.6
Latin America and the Caribbean	80,920	131,294	61.6
Middle East and North Africa	6,877	16,875	40.8
South Asia	3,722	29,185	12.8
Sub-Saharan Africa	2,877	7,649	37.6
Total	141,821	321,616	44.1

Source: The World Bank Private Participation in Infrastructure Database (http://ppi.worldbank.org)
[a] Privatization proceeds cover proceeds from concessions and divestitures.

Table 3. Top 20 Countries in Energy Privatization: 1990-2006

Ranking	Country	Total Proceeds ($ millions)	Ranking	Country	Total Proceeds ($ millions)
1	Brazil	42,819	11	Peru	3,488
2	Argentina	20,063	12	Russia	3,395
3	China	7,216	13	Chile	3,020
4	Morocco	6,607	14	India	2,982
5	Hungary	5,666	15	Poland	2,505
6	Colombia	5,349	16	Thailand	2,176
7	Czech Republic	4,906	17	Romania	2,166
8	Slovak Rep.	4,460	18	Bulgaria	2,161
9	Philippines	3,845	19	Kazakhstan	2,123
10	Malaysia	3,805	20	Dominican Rep.	1,230

Source: The World Bank Private Participation in Infrastructure Database (http://ppi.worldbank.org)

Table 3 shows the top 20 ranking of the developing and transition countries according to the privatization proceeds collected between 1990 and 2006. As Table 3 indicates, top two best performers in privatization of energy sectors are Brazil and Argentina. They are followed by China, however, the difference between proceeds of Argentina and China is nearly $13 billion. The combined share of privatization proceeds of Brazil and Argentina from energy sectors is about 44 %. This list contains six countries from Latin America/Caribbean region, eight transition economies, five countries from East/South East Asia region and one country from MENA region. This observation verifies the argument that global privatization of energy sectors has been dominated by Latin American and transition economies.

IV. "Conquest", "Robbery" and "Force Plays the Greatest Part"

IV.I "Force Plays the Greatest Part": Conditionalities

"President Reagan effectively told us to go out and make the Third World a bastion of freewheeling capitalism... Everything we did from 1983 onward was based on our new sense of mission to have the 'south' privatise or die; towards this end we created economic bedlam in Latin America and Africa in 1983-88."

Budhoo Davison, former senior manager in IMF[12]

Force, in the context of liberalization and privatization of energy sectors, has taken the form of the conditionalities imposed by international financial institutions. The World Bank defines the basic reason behind the conditionalities as: "International aid agencies (donors) typically allocate their aid resources with the expectation that the recipient country will use them in a way that is consistent with a set of objectives previously agreed between both parties. For the most part, such objectives relate to actions that are expected to improve the economic and social development of the recipient country" (World Bank, 2005a:2). According to the World Bank's review of conditionalities, the share of conditionalities related to the Financial and Private Sector development, which also covers privatization related conditionalities, increased from 30 % in the first half of the 1990s to 43 % in the second half, and then dropped to 28 % in the 2000-2004 period (World Bank, 2005b:9).[13] Hall and de la Motte indicated that the proportion of privatization related conditionalities in IMF's structural conditions rose from 4 % in the 1987-1990 period to 14 % in the 1997-1999 period. At the same time, conditionalities related to trade and exchange rate polices dropped from 30 % to 8 % (Hall and de la Motte, 2004: 5).

The World Bank and IMF attach strict sector-specific binding conditionalities to structural adjustment and project loans. These conditionalities, with a few number of exceptions, impose a mandatory restructuring of public sector. Unsurprisingly, proposed restructuring covers privatization of public enterprises. This strategy has proved to be very effective in energy sectors. As Bayliss indicates, privatization in electricity and water sectors became a strict conditionality for debt relief (Bayliss, 2002: 605). IMF delayed debt relief for Honduras for six months since the level of progress in electricity privatization was less than the institution expected (Bayliss, 2005:606). Hall and de la Motte (2004) briefly analyzed the experiences of six countries (Colombia, El Salvador, Indonesia, Mozambique, South Africa and Sri Lanka) and revealed the pressure in the form of conditionalities upon these six countries. Yi-chong gives to story of State Electricity Board (SEB) of Orissa state in India. After a resolute resistance against Bank's insistence for the reform, OSEB, finally following a serious financial strain, came to terms with the Bank and initiated a restructuring program (Yi-chong, 2005:661). After the 2001 Crisis in Turkey, the World Bank enforced an electricity market law which would pave the way for privatisations (World Bank; 2001:7). Wamukonya gives a set of illustrating examples: Bangladesh government, against the postponement of external finance, was forced to accept a power sector restructuring program by Asian development Bank and the World Bank in 1991. The financial problems of public electricity utility of Côte d'Ivoire made government contended to initiate a power sector reform of which privatization was an essential step (Wamukonya, 2003:1275). Eurodad's report underlies that Bangladesh, Burkina Faso, Nicaragua and Vietnam were prone to energy sector privatization-related conditionalities (Eurodad, 2006:13). We can also observe the same phenomenon in Europe. The EU Electricity Market Directives 1996 and 2003 (see Jamasb and Politt, 2005 for details) are also examples of international pressures and may be accepted as means of global primitive accumulation. "The Electricity Market Directive requires the breaking up of the national monopolies of the electricity supply industries, increasing transparency of accounting and the gradual opening of the electricity market to domestic and foreign competition" (Enlargement Watch, 2002:7). EBRD (European Bank for Reconstruction and Development), prior to releasing the loans for Slovakia and Ukraine, put strong pressure upon these countries to initiate power and gas sector reforms.

---

[12] Quoted by Hall and de la Motte, 2004: 5.

[13] However, an independent NGO, *Eurodad* found out that average conditionalities related to privatization attached to loans to 20 countries increased from 4 to 5 between 2002 and 2005 (Eurodad, 2006:12). According to the same report, countries under the highest number of conditionalities were Uganda (197 conditions), Nicaragua (107 conditions) and Rwanda (103 conditions) (ibid,17).

IV.2. Privatization Consultancy Firms

International financial institutions supply the necessary finance for the pre-privatization restructuring operations. These operations include hiring of some specialized firms for privatization consultancy which has been a very profitable area. These operations have channeled huge sums of money to privatization consultancy consortiums. A report by PSC and *War on Want* describes these companies as active promoters of privatization. The most important companies are Pricewaterhouse Coopers, KPMG group, Deloitte Touche Tohmatsu and ErnstYoung (PCS/ WoW, 2004). These companies have close relations with the international financial institutions.

In Ukraine, a consortium founded by Arthur Andersen, Credit Ansalt, NEKO and Union Bank of Switzerland was appointed to privatize Ukraine's largest energy companies. In Cameroon, a state-owned electricity company, SONEL was privatized through the strict surveillance of International Finances Coproration (Pineau, 2002:1004). Thai government appointed two private companies Kema Consultants and Siam Commercial Bank for consultancy in the privatization of Thai electricity sector ESI (Chirarattananon and Nirukkanaporn, 2006: 2524). In Orissa, India, the consultant firms (PricewaterhouseCoopers, KPMG and Credit Suisse) were paid over $100 million for the consultancy in the privatization of state electricity system (PCS/WW, 2004:7). Asian Development Bank estimated that, for the privatization of National Power Corporation of the Philippines required $1,715,000 for consultancy and $1,200,000 of this sum was to be financed by ADB and Japan Special Fund (ADB, 2004). Again, Asian Development Bank, supplied $1,250,000 for technical assistance in liberalization of the gas sector of Pakistan. From this budget, international and domestic consultants would be paid $660,000. By the end of 1999, total amount of privatization projects in which Pricewaterhouse Coopers was hired as the consultant firm, was totaled up to £22 billion. By the end of 2002, top five consultancy firms' portfolios covered privatization and project finance items of which total value was more than £54 billion (UNISON, 2002: 4).

IV.3. "Conquest" and "Blackmail": International Energy Companies

Strict conditionalities have broken the resistance of host countries and makes them vulnerable to the manipulation of international firms. In this setting, international energy companies have not missed any opportunity to exploit structural and economic weakness of forced-to-privatize countries. The menu of these opportunities covers a long list of legal or illegal actions ranging from blackmailing to bribery.

Enron has been the epitome of international firms benefiting from global privatization of energy sectors. It was backed by both the US government agencies and the World Bank group. The World Bank group provided $761 million between 1992 and 2001 to Enron's international operations (SEEN, 2002:4).Enron's international activities provided interesting snapshots that could testify in the favor of primitive accumulation hypothesis. For example, as SEEN report outlines, US President George W. Bush, Jr. pressured upon Argentina's president, Rudolfo Torragno to accept Enron's bid for a gas pipeline. After the election of Carlos Menem as new president of Argentina, Enron and its consortium acquired the ownership of state-owned gas pipeline in southern Argentina (SEEN, 2002:13). Enron was always very active in most of the Latin America region. This activity was always supported by the US government[14] as well: "In October 1999, in Houston, Colombian president Andrés Pastrana met with the executives of the principal oil and electricity companies in the United States, coordinated by then governor of Texas, George W. Bush. Pastrana rallied support for Plan Colombia, and promised the major oil and gas exploration concessions and the continuation of the privatization in the power sector. Enron representatives were present at this meeting with President Pastrana and Governor Bush" (SEEN, 2002:14). One other interesting example for "fair" attitude of Enron could be observed in the case of Dabhol company in Marahastra State, India. Enron owned 65 % of the company. The company decided to construct a dam at the port of Dabhol. The company planned to invest $3 billion and expected to earn $26 billion. Nevertheless, the whole project collapsed since the state electricity board bought electricity from Dabhol at 8 rupees and sold at 2 rupees per unit. Thenceforth, state electricity board could not make its payment to the company and the company stopped the project (Bayliss and Hall, 2001). However, most of the Enron's globalized energy operations were blurred by economic and political scandals, and bribery cases (as in Colombia, India, Argentina). As a rule, the countries which were supposed to be on the portfolio of Enron, received considerable loans for restructuring their energy sectors.[15]

In most of the privatization attempts or private investment projects, governments act as a guarantor (Wamukonya, 2003:1277). Therefore, private companies can afford to buy large energy assets and state acts as a mediator in this process. Besides, governments offer extra returns on assets to be privatized and these offers have been generally officialized on the privatization contracts. For example, state electricity boards, generally sign mandatory purchase agreements with privatized firms and inevitably the determined price has been very high compared to the pre-privatization period. Therefore, privatized firms gain extra profits and these agreements aggravate the financial burden of governments and electricity boards. For example, the international consortium formed by French EDF, American AES and Brazilien CSN, after appropriation Brazil's electricity retail and distribution company, Light Serviços de Electricidade, began to sell electricity at $120 /MWh while buying electricity from hydro generators at $23/MWh. At the same time EDF was charging electricity it sold to French customers at $75/ MWh (Beder, 2006: 59). The same source indicates that the states that privatized their electricity sectors were those having the highest electricity prices in Australia. In some cases, the company which appropriated the energy assets demands that the government should guarantee monopoly, as in the case of Cameroon's state-owned electricity company, SONEL. AES, the US based international firm, obtained a five year monopoly guarantee in the process of privatization of SONEL (Pineau, 2004:6). In the same contract, government became liable to provide a guaranteed profit margin.

One of the most serious charges against international energy companies is asset undervaluation. A special commission of Dominican senate announced in 2001 that the assets of the state-owned electricity company of Dominican republic, CDE, in the process of

---

[14] Enron contributed $ 1,157 thousand to 1996 election campaigns in USA
(see http://www.opensecrets.org/pubs/cashingin_electric/Enron.htm).
[15] SEEN report gives important insights about the glabalization of ENRON. "U.S. embassies in the Philippines and India helped Enron win power deals there while U.S. Ambassador Frank Wisner headed those offices from 1991 to 1994. Ambassador Wisner joined Enron's board of directors in 1997", "In 1995, with the deal apparently in jeopardy, President Clinton's National Security Advisor, Anthony Lake, reportedly held up a $13.5 million aid package, implying in a letter to Mozambican President Joaquim Chiassano that it was contingent upon affirmation of the Enron deal. President Chiassano acquiesced." (SEEN, 2002: 19).

privatization, were severely under-valued by $907 million and Enron acquired the company at 42 % of its value (SEEN, 2002: 15). In this case, Enron and the consultancy firm, Arthur Andersen was accused of cooperative fraud. In Turkey, especially in the privatization of Petkim, state-owned petrochemical producing firm, there were a lot of criticisms that the assets of the company were undervalued (Karataş, 2001:109).

The power of the international energy companies, in addition to conditionalities imposed by the World Bank, IMF and regional development banks, also comes from the flexibility of their investment portfolios. The geographical and sectoral diversification of the assets in their portfolios have increased their bargaining power. This process is also reinforced by their oligopolistic or monopolistic positions in liberalized energy sectors. This has created significant asymmetries between states and the international energy companies. We can understand the extent of regional and sectoral diversification and integration from the following quotation:

> "Through consolidations, mergers, acquisitions, and strategic alliances, the world's energy companies have also become more integrated. Oil and gas companies have become electricity companies; domestic regional electric utilities have become multinational electricity companies; electricity distribution companies have become generation companies; and generation companies have become distribution and transmission companies" (EIA, 1996).

This trend seems to be unavoidable. The privatization and liberalization policies have generated the framework for this tide. Europe is the arena in which the most mature version of this tide can be observed. Even in 2001, Sioshansi warned against the increasing tide of cross-border mergers and acquisitions in Europe and added that "the trend towards multi-utilities (e.g. electricity, gas, water, combined heat and power, district heating, waste disposal, telecommunications, environmental services, consulting etc.) is well under way" (Sioshansi, 2001:420).There are considerable asymmetries between the economic powers of countries prone to liberalization and privatization and continental and global big companies. As the report of Enlargement Watch indicated, French state-owned global player EDF bought the one third of Slovakian electricity distribution network. EDF had annual global turnover of €34.4 billion in 2000 while Slovakia's annual GDP was € 18 billion (Enlargement Watch, 2002: 35). Is there a chance for Slovakia to resist against EDF?

Table 4. Large International Energy Companies

Company	Home Country	Sectors[a]	Number of Countries
EDF	France	E, W, Ws, Tr, C,	73
AES	USA	E, W	33
Endesa	Spain	E, W, G, T	16
Enron	USA	E, W, G, M,	32
E-On	Germany	E, T, G, Ws, C, W	28
RWE	Germany	W, C, E, Ws, T, F	40
Enel	Italy	G, E, W	9

Source: Public Services International Research Unit Database (www.psiru.org)
[a] E: Electricity W: Water Ws: Waste Tr: Transport G: Gas C: Construction M: Manufacturing T: Telecommunications

Table 4 shows seven international energy companies, their regional and sectoral portfolios. As the table indicates, these companies have been operating in large number of countries. Their sectoral portfolios have displayed variations, but especially electricity and water sectors can be observed in nearly all portfolios. EDF[16] has the highest number of countries in its portfolio. These portfolios give significant clues about the flexibilization of these companies' investment strategies. In this context, it seems that states will have difficulties in opposing claims of these companies. They might be pleading for mercy from now on.

V. Conclusion

Privatization in energy sectors has proceeded with the extensive use of force, pressure and blackmail. These have also been blended with corruption and bribery. Moreover, as in the beginning of capitalism, this privatization tide is supported by an optimistic prophecy. This prophecy, at least in the context of its message, is very familiar with the prophecy whispered to the ears of freed working class in the initial phases of capitalism. Both prophecies, despite their differences, offer an emancipation. The past prophecy offered a salvation from monotonous routine work on small land holdings. The new prophecy promises to enhance living standards and reduce the burden of inefficient enterprises over society. However, two prophecies have one common feature, "force plays the greatest part" in realization of these prophecies.

Privatization in energy sectors has been accommodated by blackmail, fraud, manipulation and huge pressure; but these factors are not the reasons why we identify the contemporary process as also "primitive accumulation". We agree with the continuous primitive accumulation thesis because the basic aim of the process, the divorce of direct producers from the means of production, has been realized with the aid of these factors. Energy sector privatizations have exhibited developed versions of this process.

We should end with a question: Can capitalism survive without political power? Or is capitalism only an economic system? In the context of the transition from feudalism to capitalism, capitalism is defined as the social mode of production in which extraction of surplus has been pursued through only economic means. At the end of this study, we should ask: Is accumulation of capital not only a pure economic process but also a political process?

References

ADB [Asian Development Bank] (2004), *Proposed Technical Assistance (Financed By The Japan Special Fund) to the Republic of the Philippines for Institutional Strengthening of Energy Regulatory Commission and Privatization of National Power Corporation*, ADB.

Bayliss, K. (2000), *The World Bank and Privatisation: a Flawed Development Tool*, PSIRU/University of Cambridge, London.

Bayliss, K. (2005), "Privatization and Poverty: The Distributional Impact of Utility Privatization", *Annals of Public and Cooperative Economics*, 7(34), 603-625.

---

[16] It is interesting to note that, EDF is a state-owned company, with its partner GDF.

Bayliss, K. And D. Hall (2005), *A Corporate Contribution to Global Inequality*, PSIRU/University of Cambridge, London.

Beder, S. (2006), "Electricity: The Global Impact of Power Reforms", in *Beyond the Market: The Future of Public Services* (ed. Daniel Chavez), Amsterdam:TNI/Public Services International Research Unit (PSIRU).

Bonefeld, W. (2007), *Primitive Accumulation and Capitalist Accumulation: Economic Categories and Social Constitution*, Presentation Paper, School of Social Sciences, The University of Manchester. (http://www.socialsciences.manchester.ac.uk/disciplines/politics/research/hmrg/activities/).

Chirarattananon, S. and S. Nirukkanaporn (2006), "Deregulation of ESI and Privatization of State Electric Utilities in Thailand", *Energy Policy*, **34**, 2521-2531.

De Angelis, M. (2001), "Marx and Primitive Accumulation: The Continuous Character of Capital's 'Enclosures' ", *Commoner*, No. **2**, 1-22.

De Angelis, M. (2006), *Enclosures, Commons and the "Outside."*, Paper presented at the annual meeting of the International Studies Association, Town & Country Resort and Convention Center, San Diego, California, March 22.

EIA[Energy Information Agency] (1996), *Privatization and the Globalization of Energy Markets, Office of Energy Markets and End Use*, Washington D.C.:U.S. Department of Energy.

Enlargement Watch (2002), *The Liberalisation and Privatisation of the Gas and Electricity Sectors in Current and Prospective Member States of the European Union.*

Eurodad (2006), *World Bank and IMF Conditionality: a Development Injustice*, (www.globalpolicy.org/socecon/bwi-wto/imf/2006/06eurodadimfwb.pdf).

Grandia L. (2007), *The Tragedy of Enclosures: Rethinking Primitive Accumulation from the Guatemalan Hinterland*, Paper Presented to the Spring Colloquium, Program in Agrarian Studies, Yale University, April 27.

Hall, D. and R. De la Motte (2004), *Dogmatic Development: Privatisation and Conditionalities in Six Countries*, PSIRU/University of Cambridge, London.

Harvey, D. (2005), *New Imperialism*, New York: Oxford University Press.

Jamasb, T. and M. Politt (2005), *Electricity Market Reform in the European Union: Review of Progress toward Liberalization & Integration*, CMI Working Paper, Department Of Applied Economics, University Of Cambridge.

Karataş, C. (2001), "Privatization in Turkey: Implementation, Politics of Privatization and Perfomance Results", *Journal of International Development*, **13**, 93-121.

Kessides, I. N. (2005)," Infrastructure Privatization adn Regulation: Promises and Perils", *The World Bak research Observer*, **20**, 81-120.

Kikeri, S. and A. F. Kolo (2005), "Privatization: Trends and Recent Developments", *Policy Research Working Paper* **3765**, The World Bank.

Marx, K. (1990), *Capital I*, London: Penguin.

Moore, D. (2004), "The Second Age of the Third World: From Primitive Accumulation to Global Public Goods". *Third World Quarterly* **25**:87-109.

Newberry, D. (1997), "Privatization and Liberalization of Network Utilities", *European Economic Review*, **41**(3-5), 357-384.

PCS/WW [Public and Commercial Services Union / War on Want] (2004), *Profiting from Poverty: Privatization Consultants*, DFID and Public Services, London: War on Want.

Perelman, Michael (2007) "Primitive Accumulation from Feudalism to Neoliberalism", *Capitalism Nature Socialism*, **18**(2), 44–61.

Pineau, O.P. (2002), "Electricity Sector Reform in Cameroon: Is Privatization the Solution?", *Energy Policy*, **30**, 999-1012.

Pineau, O.P. (2004), *Transparency in the Dark–An Assessment of the Cameroonian Electricity Sector Reform*, mimeo (web.uvic.ca/padm/faculty/pineau/pdfs/cameroonassessment.pdf).

Rochlin, C. (2002), "Is Electricity a Right ?" *The Electricity Journal*, March, 31-36.

SEEN [Sustainable Energy & Economy Network] (2002), Enron's Pawns: How Public Institutions Bankrolled Enron's Globlization Game (www.seen.org).

Sioshansi, F.P. (2001), "Opportunities and Perils of the Newly Libearlized European Electricity Markets", *Energy Policy*, **29**, 419-427.

The Corner House (2000), *Exporting Corruption: Privatization, Multinationals and Bribery*, Dorset: The Corner House.

UNISON (2002), *A Web of Private Interest: How the Big Five Acccountancy Firms Influence and Profit from Privatisation Policy*, London: Unison.

Wamukonya, N. (2003), "Power Sector Reform in Developing Countries: Mismatched Agendas", *Energy Policy*, 1273-1289.

Watts, M. (2006) "Empire of Oil: Capitalist Dispossession and the Scramble for Africa", Review of the Month, *Monthly Review*, September.

World Bank (2001), *Country Assistance Strategy, Progress Report of the World Bank Group for the Republic of Turkey*, Washington D.C.:World Bank.

World Bank (2005a), *Review of World Bank Conditionality: Issues Note*, Washington D.C.: World Bank.

World Bank (2005b), *Review of World Bank Conditionality*, Washington D.C.: World Bank.

Yi-chong, X. (2005), "Models, Templates and Currents: the World Bank and Electricity Reform", *Review of International Political Economy*, **12**(4), 647–673.

In: Global Privatization and Its Impact
Editors: I.J. Hagen and T.S. Halvorsen, pp. 103-113

ISBN: 978-1-60456-785-4
© 2008 Nova Science Publishers, Inc.

Chapter 6

WHO SHALL OWN THE GENES OF FARMED FISH?

Ingrid Olesen[1], Kristin Rosendal[2], Morten Rye[3], Morten Walløe Tvedt[2] and Hans B. Bentsen[1]

[1]Nofima Marine, P.O. Box 5010, N-1432 Ås, Norway
[2] The Fridtjof Nansen Institute, P.O.Box 326, N-1326 Lysaker, Norway
[3] Akvaforsk Genetics Center, N-6600 Sunndalsøra, Norway

Abstract

Breeding companies need some form of legal or biological protection measures to assure revenues from genetic improvement and investment in genetic material. Fish farmers and fish breeders need access to genetic resources for food production and further development and sustainable use of fish genetic material. The objective of this chapter is to discuss the international and domestic legal processes and the needs of fish breeders in the aquaculture sector. For this we will review:

1.   The rationale for ensuring access to and for using legal measures for protection of breeding materials in aquaculture

2.   A Norwegian case on Norwegian salmon breeding and farming, where three dimensions that may affect choices of protection and the scope for access to fish genetic resources are considered: Awareness among fish breeders of international regulations of genetic resources; evolving structures within the aquaculture sector; technological developments and biological features presenting options and barriers

3.   The options available for protection of aquaculture genetic resources in both developed and developing countries.

Introduction

Fish breeding companies need legal protection of their genetically improved broodstock to ensure revenues from their investments in breeding and genetic improvement activities. The same players may also want access to genetic resources for further improvements and innovation. The question of how these conflicting concerns can be balanced in the aquaculture industry has recently got increasing attention and interest (Greer and Harvey,

2004; Rosendal et al., 2006; Olesen et al., 2007). In this paper, we will review and discuss the present situation and alternative regulations of protection of and access to breeding material and genetic resources in the aquaculture industry.

Background

Until about three decades ago, genetic resources including collections of wild and improved material in publicly owned gene banks, was subject to free and open access. From a legal perspective, genetic resources were largely regarded as a Common Heritage of Mankind. This status was first challenged by the evolving Plant Breeders' Rights regime and altered practices in the patent system. New biotechnologies have increasingly allowed innovations in breeding and genetics to fulfill the criteria for patent protection (Bent et al. 1987; Crespi 1988). As a consequence, there has been a shift away from the view that genetic resources are common goods and towards a situation where it is regarded as a commodity that can be privatized. At the same time it has raised concerns about misappropriation, where the intellectual property system (IP) using patenting facilitates appropriation of resources and knowledge of rural communities and developing countries. Such "bio-piracy" has been described as today's form of colonialism (Merson, 2000; Martin and Vermeylen, 2005).

In response to this development, the Convention on Biological Diversity (CBD, 1992) introduced national sovereign rights to genetic resources as an attempt to compromise between primary owners and users of these resources (Rosendal, 2000). A parallel process produced the Trade-Related aspects of Intellectual Property Rights[1] (TRIPS) agreement under the World Trade Organization (WTO), with the main objectives to harmonize, strengthen and expand the scope of intellectual property rights (IPR) protection in all technological fields. This includes biotechnology and new or improved breeding and selection methods as well as genetic engineering. TRIPS is said to promote innovation by establishing exclusive private rights to *inter alia* genetic resources through intellectual property rights, while the CBD aims at balancing the skewed distribution of biological resources and biotechnology between the North and the South (Rosendal, 2001; 2006). Besides the existing international legislation on patent law under the World Intellectual Property Organization[2] (WIPO), there are also ongoing negotiations in the Standing Committee in the WIPO for an even higher degree of international harmonization in this field (Tvedt, 2005a, pp. 311-344). In response, access regulations have been proliferating, especially among biodiversity rich, but less industrialized countries of the South.

Norway played a leadership role in the international negotiations that led to evolving norms and regulations for access and benefit sharing of genetic resources within the framework of the UN Convention of Biodiversity (CBD). Furthermore, Norway is among the first developed countries to embark on a legislative process for regulating access to these resources. According to the CBD, Norway is also responsible for the management of half of

---

[1] For details, see http://www.wto.org/english/tratop_e/trips_e/trips_e.htm
[2] The World Intellectual Property Organization is a specialized agency of the United Nations. It is dedicated to developing a balanced and accessible international intellectual property system, which rewards creativity, stimulates innovation and contributes to economic development while safeguarding the public interest. See http://www.wipo.int/about-wipo/en/what_is_wipo.html.

the world population of Atlantic salmon. Here we will therefore present a Norwegian case while also discussing it in wider global perspective where appropriate.

Norwegian Case

An interdisciplinary research team combining legal analysis, biology and political science studied the possibilities for regulating the access to genetic resources used in aquaculture (Rosendal et al., 2006). The same research team also studied the strategies of the aquaculture industry and the national and international regulations in the field (Olesen et al., 2007). This was carried out by interviewing central players within Norwegian salmon breeding and farming to study their needs and considerations with respect to such regulations. Three dimensions affecting options for access and protection of fish genetic resources were considered:
- Evolving regulations and results from interviews
- Changing structures in the aquaculture sector
- State of the art of biological and technological developments

Relevance

The topic is particularly relevant in Norway these times, because access legislation is now in the process of being developed. Today the question of property rights to genetic resources, other than intellectual property rights, is not solved in Norwegian legislation. A government appointed Expert Committee on Biodiversity proposed a new Act for Nature Diversity stating that *genetic material* is a *common resource* open for everyone to use (NOU, 2004[3]). This entails that there are no exclusive property rights to genetic material, save when the terms for intellectual property rights are fulfilled. If these principles become part of the forthcoming Nature Diversity Act, then genetic resources in Norway can be said to be in a *public domain*. However, the more recent Wild Marine Resources Act (of 6th June 2008) (NOU, 2005) demands that any utilization of marine genetic resources must go through a procedure involving the Ministry of Fisheries. However, neither the proposition nor the Wild Marine Resources Act discusses the balance between exclusive rights and access to genetic resources. Still in 2008, the question of property rights to genetic resources, other than intellectual property rights, is not solved in Norwegian legislation.

Furthermore, the issue is of current interest in Norway due to the rapidly growing aquaculture industry with particularly valuable genetic material of salmon and rainbow trout. Also, farming of Atlantic cod is now growing rapidly in Norway, and other new species (halibut, scallop etc.) are underway.

Biodiversity represents one of our most valuable resources, although this value is still hard to quantify in economic terms. Greer and Harvey (2004, p. 28) argue that "variations among wild salmon stocks will become increasingly important to the relatively new aquaculture industry as fish farmers continue to look for desirable characteristics to introduce into cultured species". In addition, the already improved Atlantic salmon genetic material represents a valuable resource for Norway, and has been one of the most important

---

[3] Norges offentlige utredninger (Norwegian Governmental Reports) NOU 2004:28, pp. 526, 634

contributions to the strong competitiveness of Norwegian salmon on the world market. The Norwegian salmon stocks, including the wild stocks, constitute valuable genetic resources that can be further developed and utilized. From this it follows that access to both wild and improved genetic resources are valuable.

Norway implemented the EU Patent Directive (Directive 98/44/EC) in 2003. Exactly what a patent under this legislation grants an exclusive right to remains to be seen, as this has not been legally tried in Norway. It also remains to be seen how patent practice will develop.

Concerns have been expressed that the Norwegian aquaculture industry may become dependent on external companies and must pay royalties for using interesting salmon genetic material originating from Norway (Gjerstad, 2000; Fish Farming International, 2000). For instance, commercial breeders may find a useful gene in a wild salmon stock, patent an isolated or modified expression of this material, and go on to demand monopoly prices from other companies that use that gene or knowledge about the gene. Patenting of genes by Norwegian players was presented as the solution to this problem. In such a scenario, commercial actors may obtain wild genetic material free of charge, due to the legal status of genetic resources being *common resources* according to the draft Nature Diversity Act or due to the lack of access regulation.

Recently, the majority of the shares (50.2%) of Norway's Aqua Gen, which is the world's largest salmon breeding company, were purchased by Germany's EW group. The EW group is the largest player in poultry genetics. The purchase was approved by the Norwegian authorities, but was heavily debated (see www.intrafish.no on i.a. January 18. 2008). The opponents held the Norwegian Seafood Federation responsible for selling a strategic important company out of the country. They were concerned that the German company will patent the genetic material developed by Norwegians and that Norwegian fish farmers have to pay high royalties to use the fish material in the future. Irrespective of patenting, Norwegian salmon multipliers and farmers may have to pay higher royalties for roe and seed from the externally controlled Aqua Gen in the future.

Survey of Norwegian Players in Fish Breeding and Farming

Olesen et al. (2007) reported that the Norwegian players in aquaculture were not very familiar with the evolving national and international norms and regulations on intellectual property rights to genetic materials or with the evolving access regulation regimes. Those who did recognize the emerging regimes, clearly stated that there must be a balance between intellectual property rights (IPR) and access regulations to prevent that vast genetic resources currently shared are being controlled commercially by a few companies. Their experiences were that these regulations were highly complex and currently of low relevance for most players in fish breeding. Furthermore, strict regulations were considered to severely limit the developments in this field, because few players has the size and economic strength to pursue key patents and thus limit and possibly exclude activity by the many small and economically vulnerable players in the sector today.

Market consolidations and privatization are among the factors that the companies themselves recognized as most important in changing the ground rules within the sector. Even though the similar history of the plant and agricultural sector does not seem to have a high visibility among the relevant players, most are becoming more concerned with the questions of access to and protection of the wild and improved breeding material that is central to their trade. This realization is predominantly linked to external use of Norwegian salmon genetic resources, as most breeders are still confident in the superiority of their own breeding lines. Nevertheless, the breeders also acknowledged their vulnerability, should access to new and improved materials or traits become severely restricted.

Alternative Biological and Legal Protection Mechanisms and How to Balance Access Regimes

The legal protection of the use of genetically improved plant varieties has been regulated through Plant Breeders Rights within the International Union for the Protection of New Varieties of Plants (UPOV). Plant breeders' rights are based on characterization of *new, distinct, uniform and stable* varieties, i.e. phenotypic and/or genetically uniform populations. Access or exchange of fish genetic resources and forms of legal protection of investments or research on these resources in aquaculture have, however, not been addressed extensively (Greer and Harvey, 2004), although there are important differences between plant and fish populations in terms of phenotypic and genetic characterization. Plant populations, and in particular commercial plant varieties, are often formed as a result of homogenizing processes like inbreeding and vegetative propagation. Accumulation of inbreeding does not seem to impair the viability and performance of plant populations as it normally does in animal populations. Breeding programs for fish normally aim at minimizing inbreeding and maintaining genetic variation within the population. Hence, the populations will not be uniform and stable, but variable and evolving from generation to generation.

Legal and biological aspects relating to various options of biological and legal protection of aquaculture genetic resources are discussed by Rosendal et al. (2006) and Olesen et al (2007). Until now, most animal breeding programs have relied on various biologically based strategies to encourage the users of their genetic material to deal directly with the program.

Biological Protection Strategies

The most common strategy in aquaculture breeding programs is continuous upgrading of the genetic quality of its material to maintain competitive power and hence make the customers come back regularly for new purchases. Still, the buyer may, of course, reproduce the material without the knowledge of the supplier, and it will have to be considered as *de facto* free-access material. Hence, it will be difficult for a superior program to gain a large competitive advantage, since other programs may hitchhike (though with some delay) on its genetic progress. This may increase the focus by the breeding programs on marketing and service/support rather than on increasing the genetic progress.

Crossbreeding and hybrids are widely applied in many plant species, because it is relatively easy to produce a large number of inbred lines and to identify crossbreds that express significant heterosis effects. The heterosis effects will be gradually lost in progeny generations, and denying access to the parent lines will protect them from piracy. In aquaculture breeding, applied crossbreeding programs are however scarce due to problems with inbreeding depression and high costs of developing/keeping parent lines and combining crossing and selection.

Use of sterile fish in aquaculture will prevent unauthorized propagation efficiently. In several aquaculture species, applicable methods based on polyploidy are available for commercial-scale propagation of sterile production animals (Pepper, 1991; Sutterlin and Collier, 1991, Felip et al., 2001, Nell, 2002). These are routinely used in some production systems today (Bonnet et al., 1999; Nell, 2002) to avoid problems with sexual maturation and spawning. The methods have not been widely applied in salmon farming due to consumer skepticism to chromosome manipulated organisms and undesirable side effects of triploidy on productivity (lower growth and yields as reported by O'Flynn et al., 1997).

Legal Protection Strategies

Legal protection measures include branding, material transfer agreements (MTA), patenting, and a *sui generis* system for aquaculture. Traditionally, the approach for seeking legal property rights for genetically improved populations of fish has been to register product names and trademarks. Strictly, this will not protect the genetic material from being propagated and used by outsiders, but only prevent unauthorized use of the registered name. Branding can be combined with additional measures such as biological protection strategies like continuous upgrading or crossbreeding of the material, or with high quality management of the seed production process, good customer support and services, and high profile information and marketing strategies. Then the customers may find safety and production benefits from returning to the branded sources. The Norwegian players referred to by Olesen et al. (2007) seemed to conceive this strategy as the most relevant for the current situation although it does not hamper access to genetic material for further research and development unless it is combined with MTAs.

Private legal contracts (Material transfer agreements; MTA) between seller and buyer have traditionally been the most common means for regulating trade and transfer of livestock. Here, the breeding program supplies the user with genetically improved broodstock or seeds, often via a multiplier, on conditions involving e.g. financial returns to the breeding program and limitations on the use of the material. Possible financial benefits arising from a successful and competitive strategy in the breeding nucleus may be partly channeled back from multipliers through a contracted royalty fee on each egg or juvenile sold. However, the experience with this type of MTAs among some of our respondents was mixed. There have been problems with control, enforcement and monitoring of the terms of the agreements with the multipliers, and instances of contract violations have occurred. One problem seems to be the difficulties in tracing and verifying the number and origin of marketed seed. Another challenge is that it is only legally binding for the two parties signing the agreement and not for any third parties. To secure investments in breeding, this approach must be combined with strong rules on restricting further distribution of the material and improved tracing opportunities.

Patenting is one of the strongest protection measures. To be granted a patent, the invention must fulfill the patent criteria; it must be regarded *novel*, involve a sufficient level of *inventive step* and have a use (*industrially applicable*). The invention to be patented may entail either a product or a process related to biological material. If the process combines a biological process only with a very low level of technological, non-biological knowledge, it can also be patented. This will probably be the most common case for patents in the fish breeding sector, as the pure biological processes, such as selection and crossbreeding, will be known to everyone and thus form a part of the *prior art*. One reason why patents have not been applied extensively to the aquaculture sector might be that it is difficult to fulfill the patent criteria. This might be due to lack of knowledge about which gene variants or genotypes are present in superior animals. Genes may directly or indirectly be patented through e.g. patents on a gene sequence, major gene affecting an important trait, a genetic marker, a method for identifying a genetic marker or a transgenic animal. A scan of Norwegian fish patents in 2007 only revealed three such patents, one involved a genetic marker for disease resistance (Patent NO 317342) and two on transgenic fish (patent NO 321650 and application NO 20064420) (Olesen et al., 2007). Thus, increased knowledge about the genome of each fish species will increase the applicability of the patent system for protecting the commercial use of such knowledge. Gene technology may reduce the barriers to patenting inventions, but has so far not been much applied in animal breeding in spite of high expectations for a long period. Another problem with patenting genes in breeding populations may be the long time from application to granting a patent, while there is a continuous genetic improvement from selection programs. For species with short generation intervals, a moderate non-recurrent genetic improvement by a gene exchange or transfer may be passed over by a couple of generations of selection in a modern breeding program. Hence, patents affecting the fish breeding options severely may either be related to genes with large effects on important traits, as e.g. patents on the gene itself or on technical processes on selecting for such genes, (via e.g. marker genes linked to it, so called marker assisted selection, MAS). For instance, high rates of royalties for getting access to a gene variant (allele) or for using a technology for selecting for (increasing frequency of) the allele may prohibit other smaller breeding companies from choosing specific efficient breeding strategies (e.g. MAS). The MAS technology may also be of temporary value if it concerns only one specific gene, because it will be irrelevant when the favorable gene variant eventually reaches fixation in the target population. Patented transgenic fish must also show long-term competitive benefits with respect to consumer price (production cost) and product quality in order to affect breeders' options for access and protection significantly. If so, transgenic technology will facilitate protection through patenting in the same way as other gene technology mentioned above.

The risks of the patent law in the traditional breeding with competition between patent holders and traditional breeders have also been focused (Noiville, 1999, Rye, 2000). For example, a company may sell genetically modified animals without the breeders' permission to use their genetic material (breed, strain or stock). Other problems arise from very broad patents (further discussed below). Rye (2000) also stressed the problem of the lack of legal mechanisms for sharing the benefits between a patent holder and the breeder or owner developing the fish population from which the patented gene or animal originated. From an ideal perspective, the scope of the protection should encompass all that the inventor has added to the state of the art, but nothing more. If it covers more than the addition to the state of the art, the patent protection is too broad. It is assumed that *broad patents* may severely hamper access to breeding stocks, as this will make its use too costly for smaller companies. Similarly, if there are many patents in one field of technology, it may become difficult and costly for new inventors to obtain licenses from all patent holders. Such practical and monetary obstacles may hinder the development of new inventions in a technical field. The problems of misappropriation resulting from patenting, bio-piracy and practice of patenting of spurious "inventions" with lack of novelty and inventive step has also been addressed by Hoare and Tarasofsky (2007). These authors concluded that it will be difficult to design patent rules that are effective in preventing misappropriation of genetic resources until fundamental debates on the role and scope of the IP system are concluded. Should an IP system be a tool to ensure equitable practice, or is this outside the scope of such system? They also raise fundamental questions to the recent trends with broadening in scope of patents, lowering novelty requirements and advances in technology and what kind of products should be patentable. It is suggested that other policy instruments than disclosure of origin of the genetic resources may be more effective in ensuring equitable benefits while not hindering access and research. Other options such as use of existing legal principles within the patent law (doctrine of "unclean hands", rules on inventions that are contrary to *ordre public* and morality, raising the bar with respect to the degree of innovation required by an inventor) and other mechanisms (e.g. use of competition law, international legal cooperation and some kind of a liability regime).

Patenting has also been recommended as a preventive strategy to prevent others from patenting the same invention (Fish Farming International, 2000; Gjerstad, 2000). This is, however, a costly and by no means secure strategy. To publish the new invention or new knowledge may be a better strategy, as it brings the knowledge into the public domain and thus prevents others from patenting it. The use of patents in a breeding program is a very costly process, both in terms of achieving and enforcing the patent. This strategy may be best suited for larger companies within a technological sector.

Even if the patent system is applicable for the fish breeding sector and facilitates the strongest protection, there are essential legal and biological barriers linked to patenting as a strategy for securing investments in fish genetic improvement programs. Gene transfer and other gene modifications could provide a strong protection mechanism to aid enforcement, but this strategy is hardly compatible with restrictive Norwegian and some EU-countries' views on genetically modified animals.

Romstad and Stokstad (2005) discussed market power and patenting of genetic resources. When the degree of monopoly increases as a result from patenting, the possibility to provide the products for a price larger than the production cost increases. Furthermore, the use of market power and cost of exclusion can make private provision less efficient than an ideal public provision.

There are still no Animal Breeders' Rights similar to plant breeders' rights (PBR) in the UPOV system. There are however international processes looking at such possibilities. The difficult question is how such a system could be designed. The major danger in this process is that such a system would borrow or use experiences from the plant sector without taking sufficiently into account the special features of the fish breeding and farming sector. As mentioned, most fish breeding systems are dependent on heterogeneous populations and hence unsuited to fulfill the plant breeders' rights criteria of *new, distinct, uniform* and *stable*. Perhaps this reflects a need for a specially adapted type of intellectual property system for aquaculture breeds. In legal terms this is called a *sui generis* system. Such a system should address such issues as what can be protected, criteria for obtaining protection and the extent of exclusive rights that can be obtained.

Other Protection Methods

Trade secrets are also used to protect inventions. Trade secrets do not guarantee an exclusive right in a similar manner as does a patent. Because the product (the commercial seed) in aquaculture may usually be copied without knowledge about the trade secrets, simply by growing and reproducing the animals, secrecy about the procedures will not alone provide exclusivity to the genetic material resulting from the activities.

Trade secrets with large effects are bound to attract attention and attempts at copying, and competitors may even patent the leaked secret. Altogether, trade secrets are a rather insecure strategy to ensure a monopoly right in the aquaculture context.

Another method to get control of external markets is heavy lobbying through high level channels in governmental agencies in the target country to introduce specific mandatory requirements to the organisms used in aquaculture. One recent example involving crustaceans is the requirements established by several Asian countries of allowing introductions of only Specific Pathogen Free (SPF) (Lightner, 2005) certified stocks of shrimps, which in consequence "monopolies" these markets to few companies offering SPF certified stocks. This happens in spite of the fact that the SPF status is strictly limited to pathogens listed in the actual SPF list used for certification, and that it does not provide information about the animals' genetic qualities for any trait, including its ability to resist pathogens that the animals encounter in the new production environments. Hence stocks with strong innate resistance to relevant pathogens may be excluded from the new markets due to lack of SPF status.

Enforcement

A critical issue for enforcement of many protection methods is the possibility to control illegal use and document the origin of e.g. fish produced or reproduced illegally. Rosendal et al. (2006) described different methods based on gene technology and molecular biology, and concluded that DNA fingerprinting/profiling and certificates of origin were considered the most relevant for documenting the origin of fish reproduced illegally. Consumers' demand for traceable products may give food products a competitive advantage if they can be traced back to breeding programs with a documented practice that is conceived as clean, natural and environmental friendly. In an international context, national regulations that ensure traceability all the way back to the breeding nucleus may also increase the competitiveness of the national industry. To be accepted as reliable, certificates of the fish origin need to be verifiable. For this purpose, tracing by DNA fingerprinting may be a feasible technology. It would require that tissue samples are collected, frozen and stored from all commercial broodstock in the breeding nucleus and at the hatcheries. If the certificates include information about the genetic origin of the broodstock used to produce the commercial seed, verification by DNA fingerprinting would be affordable, because a limited number of tissue samples need to be analyzed. The trace system may then be used to ensure that the breeder receives royalties according to the material transfer agreement for the use of their brood stock. It may be relatively easy to establish such a system on the national level, but an international system will be rather challenging to initiate and enforce.

Conclusion

A most significant finding is that there is a discrepancy between the knowledge of farmers and breeders with respect to access and legal rights to genetic resources and the actual possibilities and limits offered by today's and forthcoming legislation. In order to maximize the aquaculture industries' potential, there is an evident need for information about access and legal rights to genetic resources. A possible public domain regulation will likely increase the possibility for access to wild genetic resources.

The predominant view in the Norwegian aquaculture industry is that the sector needs to find a balance between access to breeding material and protection of own innovations in fish breeding. Coupled with this view is an emerging realization that the value of improved breeding material is invariably underestimated, leaving the farmers (during the peaks in the market) to reap most of the added value from fish breeding and farming.

Against this background, an interest in finding some way of capturing the value of the improved stocks is emerging among the fish breeders. During an evaluation of protection mechanisms, it can be concluded that all face different problems in finding a balance between verification and feasibility (strong and not too costly protection) on the one side and access for other breeders and maintaining genetic variability on the other.

References

Bent, S.A., Schwaab, R.L., Conlin, D.G., Jeffery, D.D., 1987. *Intellectual Property Rights in Biotechnology Worldwide*. Stockton Press, US and Canada.

Bonnet S., Haffray, P., Blanc, J.M., 1999. Genetic variation in growth parameters until commercial size in diploid and triploid freshwater rainbow trout (Oncorhynchus mykiss) and seawater brown trout (Salmo trutta). *Aquaculture* **173**, 359-375

Crespi, R.S., 1988. *Patents: a Basic Guide to Patenting in Biotechnology*. Cambridge: Cambridge University Press, Cambridge.

Felip, A., Piferrer, F., Carrillo, M., Zanuy, S., 2001 A comparison of the gonadal development and plasma levels of sex steroid hormones in diploid and triploid sea bass. *J. Exp. Zool.* **290**, 384-395

Fish farming International, 2000. Patent plans for salmon. *Fish farming International*, May 2000, p 46.

Gjerstad, T., 2000. "Ta patent på laksen!" ("Patent the salmon!"). Interview by Gjerstad with Lars Aukrust, Norwegian Research Council, in Dagbladet (Norwegian daily newspaper) 16 April 2000. http://www.dagbladet.no/nyheter/2000/04/16/201409.html Accessed 25 January 2008

Greer, D., Harvey, B., 2004. *Blue Genes*. Sharing and Conserving the World's Aquatic Genetic Resources. Earthscan, London. 231 pp.

Hoare, A.L., Tarasofsky, R. 2007. *Patenting genetic resources: Striving for the right balance. Briefing paper*. Chatham House, London, October 2007. 8 pp.

Lightner, D. 2005. Biosecurity in Shrimp Farming: Pathogen exclusion through use of SPF stock and routine surveillance. *Journal of the World Aquaculture Society* **36**: 229-248.

Martin, G. and Vermeylen, S.. 2005. Intellectual property, indigenous knowledge, and biodiversity. *Capitalism Nature Socialism* **16**: 27-48.

Merson, J. 2000. Bioprospecting or Bio-Piracy: Intellectual property rights and biodiversity in a colonial and postcolonial context. *Osiris* **15:** 282-296.

Nell, J.A., 2002. Farming triploid oysters. *Aquaculture* **210**, 69-88.

NOU (Norwegian Governmental Reports). 2004. *Draft Norwegian Nature Diversity Act.* Norwegian Ministry of Environment. NOU 2004:28.

NOU (Norwegian Governmental Reports). 2005. *Draft Wild Marine Resources Act.* Norwegian Ministry of Fisheries. NOU 2005:10.

O'Flynn, F.M., McGeachy, S.A., Friars, G.W., Benfey, T.J., Bailey, J.K., 1997. Comparisons of cultured triploid and diploid Atlantic salmon (*Salmo salar*). *ICES J. Mar. Sci.* **54**, 1160-1165.

Olesen, I., Rosendal, G.K., Walløe Tvedt, M., Bryde, M, Bentsen, H.B.. 2007. Access to and protection of aquaculture genetic resources - Strategies and regulations. *Aquaculture* **272S1**: 47-61 .

Pepper, V.A., 1991. Production of non-maturing salmonids: motives, actions and goals using Newfoundland region as a model. In: V.A. Pepper (Editor), Proceedings of the Atlantic Canada Workshop on Methods for the Production of Non-Maturing Salmonids. *Can. Tech. Rep. Fish. Aquat. Sci,* **1789**, 101-109.

Romstad, E., Stokstad, G., 2005. Valuation of genetic resources. Report for Norwegian Council of Genetic Resources, P.O. Box. 5003, N-1432 Ås, Norway. 42 pp.

Rosendal, G.K., 2000. *The Convention on Biological Diversity and Developing Countries.* Kluwer Academic Publishers, Dordrecht, the Netherlands.

Rosendal, G.K., 2001. Impacts of overlapping international regimes: The case of biodiversity. *Global Governance.* **7**, 95-117.

Rosendal, G.K., 2006. The CBD and TRIPS: Different approaches to access and benefit sharing relating to genetic resources – diverging behavioral interaction? In: Oberthür, S., Gehring, T. (Eds.), Institutional Interaction: Enhancing Cooperation and Preventing Conflicts Between International and European Environmental institutions. MIT Press, Cambridge.

Rosendal, G.K., Olesen, I., Bentsen, H.B., Walløe Tvedt, M., Bryde, M., 2006. Access and legal protection of aquaculture genetic resources - Norwegian Perspectives. *The Journal of World Intellectual Property* **9**: 392-412.

Rye, M., 2000. Bipatenter – mulige konsekvenser for genetisk foredlingsarbeid i akvakultur. In: Rogne S., Borge, O.J. (Eds.), Biopatenter og EUs patentdirektiv. Rapport Åpent møte 29 September 2000. *Bioteknologinemnda*, Oslo, pp 26-27

Sutterlin, A.M., Collier, C., 1991. Some observations on commercial use of triploid rainbow trout and Atlantic salmon in Newfoundland, Canada. In: V.A. Pepper (Editor), Proceedings of the Atlantic Canada Workshop on Methods for the Production of Non-Maturing Salmonids. *Can. Tech. Rep. Fish. Aquat. Sci.* **1789**: 88-96.

Tvedt, M.W., 2005. How will a substantive patent law treaty affect the public domain for genetic resources and biological material? *The Journal of World Intellectual Property* **3**, 311–344.

Chapter 7

QUANTITATIVE ANALYSIS OF PRIVATIZATION

M. Vahabi and G.R. Jafari
Department of Physics, Shahid Beheshti University,
Evin, Tehran 19839, Iran

Abstract

In recent years, the economic policy of privatization, which is defined as the transfer of property or responsibility from public sector to private sector, is one of the global phenomenon that increases use of markets to allocate resources. One important motivation for privatization is to help develop factor and product markets, as well as security markets. Progress in privatization is correlated with improvements in perceived political and investment risk. Many emerging countries have gradually reduced their political risks during the course of sustained privatization. In fact, most risk resolution seems to take place as privatization proceeds to its later stage. Alternative benefits of privatization are improved risk sharing and increased liquidity and activity of the market. One of the main methods to develop privatization is entering a new stock to the markets for arising competition. However, attention to the capability of the markets to accept a new stock is substantial. Without considering the above statement, it is possible to reduce the market's efficiency. In other words, introduction of a new stock to the market usually decreases the stage of development and activity and increases the risk. Based on complexity theory, we quantify how the following factors: stage of development, activity, risk and investment horizons play roles in the privatization.

1. Introduction

In recent years, economics and finance have been at the focus of many researchers in various fields. Among these researchers, physicists, Mathematicians and engineers attempt to apply existing knowledge from mathematics' approaches to economic problems [1, 2, 3, 4, 5, 6, 7, 8, 9]. The aim is to characterize the statistical properties of given markets time series with the hope to provide useful information to create new models able to reproduce experimental facts.

In economics, a financial market is a mechanism that allows people to participate as investors and easily buy and sell financial securities, commodities, etc at low transaction costs and at prices. In fact, producers have obtained a feed back from consumers. This is because consumers are their investors and their benefits lies in the development and success of the markets. In finance, financial markets facilitate the raising of capital (in the capital markets), the transfer of risk (in the derivatives markets) and international trade (in the currency markets). Among various economic problems, privatization has been an interesting one for many researchers [10, 11, 12, 13, 14, 15, 16, 17, 18, 19, 20, 21]. Nowadays, the economic policy of privatization, which is defined as the transfer of property or responsibility from government to business, is a matter of interest in many countries. We assume that the goal of government is to promote efficiency. Indeed, it is now quite difficult to find a country that has not embarked on a program to involve the private sector in their management, ownership, and financing. Even if privatization processes seem to pursue a common global trend, the extent of divestiture varies greatly across countries. In some countries, governments have followed a consistent and continuous privatization policy as a part of wider reform packages, while in some others, it has been sporadic and small-scaled [12]. However, there is no doubt that privatization has had a major impact on capital markets and trading volumes. Privatization can range from a simple contract with a private vendor to the sale of a public asset. There are many reasons why governments turn to privatization. Cost reduction is one motivation for privatization. The desire to transfer risk from the public sector to the private sector can lead to privatization. A higher level of service and an absence of expertise within the governmental unit can also be another reasons. The time frame with which a project needs to be completed could also factor in the decision for privatization. A final potential reason for privatization is the flexibility provided by the private sector. One of the methods for privatization is share issue privatization. In this method, the government sells shares of the government run company which can then be traded on various stock markets, though a developed secondary market is necessary [22]. Indeed, financial market development is mentioned as one of the primary objectives of privatization. A remarkable wealth of evidence shows the correlation between financial market development and privatization. Yet, stock markets develop also in the absence of privatization [11]. Proponents of privatization believe that private market actors can more efficiently deliver any good or service that government can provide. Privatization proponents' faith in the market is philosophically based on an economic principle of competition: where there is a profit to be made, competition will inevitably arise, and that competition will inevitably draw prices down while increasing efficiency and quality. However, some would point out that privatizing certain functions of government might hamper coordination, and charge firms with specialized and limited capabilities to perform functions which they are not suited for.

It has been clear in the transition economies that the success of the privatization program depends on the strength of the markets within the same country, and vice versa. Thus, the impact of privatization will differ across countries depending on the strength of the existing private sector. Similarly, the evidence suggests that the effectiveness of privatization depends on institutional factors, such as the protection of investors. However, privatization can also stimulate the development of institutions that improve the operations of markets. A key decision to be made by the privatizing government is the method through which the state-owned asset is transferred to private ownership. This decision is difficult because, in addition to the economic factors such as valuing the assets, privatization is generally part of an ongoing, highly politicized process. Some of the factors that influence the privatization method include: (1) the history of the assets ownership, (2) the need to pay off important interest groups in the privatization, (3) the capital market conditions and existing institutional framework for corporate governance in the country, (4) the sophistication of potential investors, and, (5) the governments willingness to let foreigners own divested assets [23]. The complexity of the goals of the process means that different countries have used many different methods for privatizing various types of assets. Although financial economists have learned much about selling assets in well-developed capital markets, we still have a limited understanding of the determinants and the implications of the privatization method for state-owned assets. Theoreticians have modeled some aspects of the privatization process but, to be tractable, their models must ignore important factors. Empirical evidence on the determinants of privatization is also limited by the complexity of the goals of the privatization process.

Progress in privatization is correlated with improvements in perceived political risk. These gains tend to be gradual over the privatization period and are significantly larger in privatizing countries than in non-privatizing countries, suggesting that the resolution of such risk is endogenous to the privatization process. Changes in political risk in general tend to have a strong effect on local stock market development and excess returns in emerging economies, suggesting that political risk is a priced factor. The resolution of political risk resulting from successful privatization has been an important source for the rapid growth of stock markets in emerging economies. The recent wave of privatization sales in developing countries should have altered the perceived political risks of these countries considerably, especially if governments have successfully implemented the announced privatization plans. Such shifts in political risk tend to affect the attractiveness of equity investments and are therefore related to stock market development. Many emerging countries have gradually reduced their political risks during the course of sustained privatization. In fact, most risk resolution seems to take place as privatization proceeds to its later stage. The known benefits of privatization are reduction in public debt, improved incentives and efficiency, and better access to capital [24].

We relate how privatization depends on stock market development. Furthermore, liquidity, rather than capitalization, provides incentives for information acquisition to financial analysts. Based on recent researches, concepts of high activity and degree of development and low risk of the markets have been defined [25, 26, 27, 28, 29]. Some reports indicate that [28, 29] Level Crossing (LC) and Hurst exponent show remarkable differences between developed and emerging markets. Level Crossing analysis is very sensitive to correlation when the time series is shuffled and to probability density functions (PDF) with fat tails when the time series is surrogated.

2. Level Crossing Analysis

Let us consider a time series $\{p(t)\}$, of price index with length n, and the price returns $r(t)$ which is defined by $r(t) = \ln p(t + 1) - \ln p(t)$.

Let for a typical time interval T, ν_α^+ denotes the number of positive difference crossings $r(t) - \bar{r} = \alpha$ in time t (see figure 1) and let the mean value for all the time intervals be $N_\alpha^+(T)$ where [30]:

$$N_\alpha^+(T) = E[n_\alpha^+(T)]. \tag{1}$$

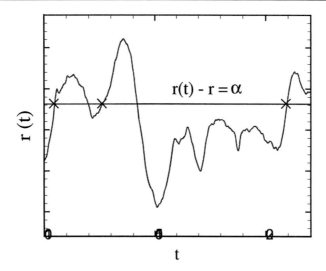

Figure 1. Schematic positive slope crossings in a fixed level, α.

In other words, ν_α^+ is the average frequency of positive slope crossings of the level α.

For the homogeneous process, if we take a second interval of T immediately following the first we shall obtain the same result, and for the two intervals together we shall therefore obtain [30]

$$N_\alpha^+(2T) = 2N_\alpha^+(T), \tag{2}$$

from which it follows that, for a homogeneous process, the average number of crossings is proportional to the time interval T. Hence

$$N_\alpha^+(T) \propto T, \tag{3}$$

or

$$N_\alpha^+(T) = \nu_\alpha^+ T. \tag{4}$$

which ν_α^+ is the average frequency of positive slope crossings of the level $r(t) - \bar{r} = \alpha$. We now consider how the frequency parameter ν_α^+ can be deduced from the underlying probability distributions for $r(t) - \bar{r}$. Consider a time scale Δt of a typical sample function, if $r(t) - \bar{r} < \alpha$ at time t and $r(t) - \bar{r} > \alpha$ at $t + \Delta t$ or alternatively the changes in r(t) is positive in the time interval Δt, there will be a positive crossing of $r(t) - \bar{r} = \alpha$,

$$r(t) - \bar{r} < \alpha \quad and \quad \frac{\Delta(r(t) - \bar{r})}{\Delta t} > \frac{\alpha - (r(t) - \bar{r})}{\Delta t}. \tag{5}$$

Actually what we really mean is that there will be high probability of a crossing in interval Δt if these conditions are satisfied [30].

In order to determine whether the above conditions are satisfied at any arbitrary location t, we must find how the values of $y = r - \bar{r}$ and $y' = \frac{\Delta y}{\Delta t}$ are distributed by considering their joint probability density $p(y, y')$. Suppose that the level $y = \alpha$ and interval Δt are specified. Then we are only interested in values of $y < \alpha$ and values of $y' = (\frac{\Delta y}{\Delta t}) > \frac{\alpha - y}{\Delta t}$

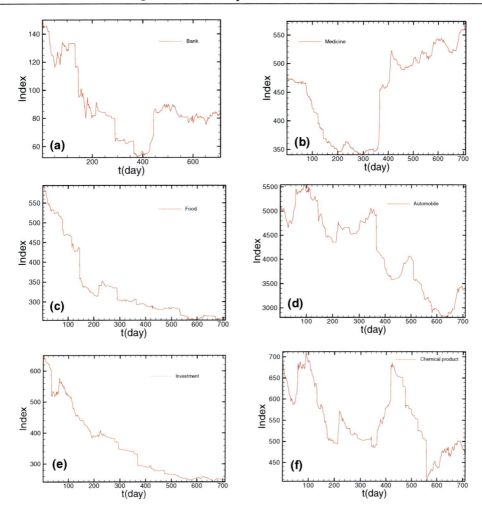

Figure 2. Indices history (Jan. 2005 - Mar. 2008) of some TEPIX subgroups (a) Bank, (b) Medicine, (c) Food, (d) Automobile, (e) Investment and (f) Chemical products.

, which means that the region between the lines $y = \alpha$ and $y' = \frac{\alpha - y}{\Delta t}$ in the plane (y, y'). Hence the probability of positive slope crossing of $y = \alpha$ in Δt is [30]:

$$\int_0^\infty \Delta y' \int_{\alpha - y' \Delta t}^\alpha \Delta y p(y, y'). \tag{6}$$

When $\Delta t \to 0$, it is legitimate to put

$$p(y, y') = p(y = \alpha, y'). \tag{7}$$

Since at large values of y and y' the probability density function approaches zero fast enough, therefore eq.(6) may be written as [30]:

$$\int_0^\infty dy' \int_{\alpha - y' dt}^\alpha dy p(y = \alpha, y') \tag{8}$$

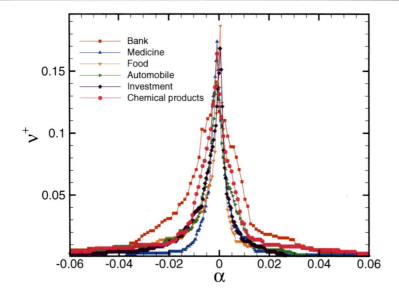

Figure 3. Comparison of the positive Level Crossings of some TEPIX subgroup indices.

in which the integrand is no longer a function of y so that the first integral is just: $\int_{\alpha - y'dt}^{\alpha} dy p(y = \alpha, y') = p(y = \alpha, y')y'dt$, so the probability of slope crossing of $y = \alpha$ in dt is equal to [30]:

$$dt \int_0^{\infty} p(\alpha, y')y'dy' \tag{9}$$

in which the term $p(\alpha, y')$ is the joint probability density $p(y, y')$ evaluated at $y = \alpha$.

We have said that the average number of positive slope crossings in scale T is $\nu_{\alpha}^{+}T$, according to (4). The average number of crossings in interval dt is therefore $\nu_{\alpha}^{+}dt$. So, average number of positive crossings of $y = \alpha$ in interval dt is equal to the probability of positive crossing of $y = a$ in dt, which is only true because dt is small and the process $y(t)$ is smooth so that there cannot be more than one crossing of $y = \alpha$ in time interval dt, therefore we have $\nu_{\alpha}^{+}dt = dt \int_0^{\infty} p(\alpha, y')y'dy'$, from which we get the following result for the frequency parameter ν_{α}^{+} in terms of the joint probability density function $p(y, y')$

$$\nu_{\alpha}^{+} = \int_0^{\infty} p(\alpha, y')y'dy'. \tag{10}$$

Some authors have used other forms for ν_{α}^{+} which are as follows [31]:

$$\nu_{\alpha}^{+} = P(y_i > \alpha, y_{i-1} < \alpha) \tag{11}$$

$$\begin{aligned} \nu_{\alpha}^{+} &= \int_{-\infty}^{\alpha} \int_{\alpha}^{\infty} P(y_i, y_{i-1}) dy_i dy_{i-1} \\ &= \int_{-\infty}^{\alpha} \int_{\alpha}^{\infty} P(y_i|y_{i-1}) P(y_{i-1}) dy_i dy_{i-1} , \end{aligned} \tag{12}$$

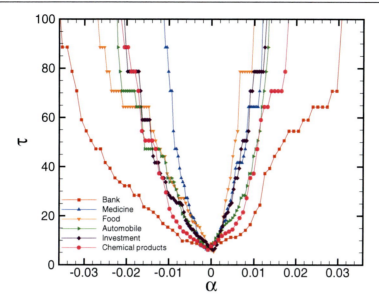

Figure 4. Comparison of the waiting time of some TEPIX subgroup indices.

Let us also use the quantity $N_{tot}^+(q)$ as [28]

$$N_{tot}^+(q) = \int_{-\infty}^{+\infty} \nu_\alpha^+ |\alpha - \bar{\alpha}|^q d\alpha. \tag{13}$$

where zero moment (with respect to ν_α^+) $q = 0$, shows the total number of crossings for price returns with positive slope. The moments $q < 1$ give information about the frequent events while moments $q >> 1$ are sensitive for the tail of events.

LC analysis is very sensitive to correlation when the time series is shuffled and to probability density functions (PDF) with fat tails when the time series is surrogated. To study the effects of correlations and probability density functions (PDF), we have evaluated N_{sh}^+ (which is the total number of positive-slope crossings of the height fluctuation series when it is shuffled) and N_{su}^+ (which is the total number of positive-slope crossings of the series when it is surrogated). The shuffling and surrogating procedures are explained in the following:

2.1. Shuffling Procedure

A celebrated theorem of Aldous, Bayer, and Diaconis asserts that it takes $\frac{3}{2}\log_2 n$ riffle shuffles to randomize a deck of n cards, asymptotically for large n, and that the randomization occurs abruptly according to a cutoff phenomenon. Shuffling by random transpositions is one of the simplest random walks on the symmetric group: given n cards in a row, at each step two cards are picked uniformly at random and exchanged. This shuffle was precisely analyzed in 1981 [32]. We have used random transpositions for shuffling our data. The long range correlations are destroyed by the shuffling procedure. As it will be pointed, in liquid markets, correlations of returns are small and in inefficient markets correlations are large. Hence, by comparing the original returns with the shuffled ones we can obtain the

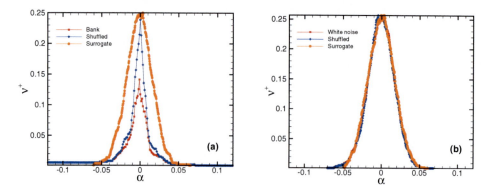

Figure 5. Typical comparison of the positive Level Crossings of bank index, its shuffled & surrogate with a white noise (the standard deviations of the curves are the same).

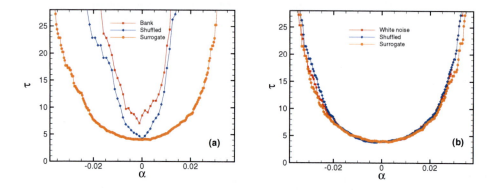

Figure 6. Typical comparison of the waiting times of bank index, its shuffled & surrogate with a white noise (the standard deviations of the curves are the same).

magnitude of correlations in the market and this can help us gain useful information about the market.

2.2. Surrogating Procedure

Another procedure that is used for obtaining valuable information about the time series is surrogating procedure. In the surrogate method surrogates are generated by replacing the true phases with a set of pseudo independent distributed uniform $(-\pi, +\pi)$ generated by any good pseudorandom uniform subroutines [33]. The phase of the discrete Fourier transform coefficients of time series are replaced with a set of pseudo-independent distributed uniform $(-\pi, +\pi)$ quantities generated by any good pseudorandom uniform subroutines. The correlations in the surrogate series do not change, but the probability function changes to Gaussian distribution [33, 34, 35, 36, 37, 38, 29]. The main objective is to provide a kind of baseline or control against which the original data can be compared. The physical idea behind the surrogates method is that a nonlinear operation on a stationary random forcing process generates cross frequency coupling between complex amplitudes. The discrete Fourier transform (DFT) of the observed time series data is computed and then the phases

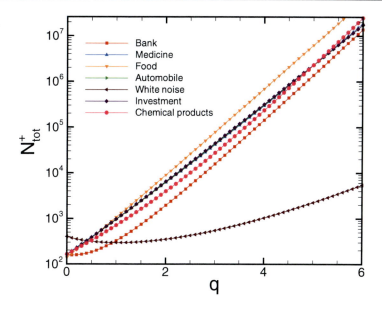

Figure 7. Generalized total number of crossings with positive slope $N_{tot}^+(q)$ for some TEPIX subgroup indices.

of each complex amplitude of the DFT are replaced with independently distributed artificial uniform $(-\pi, +\pi)$ variates. The altered DFT is then inverse Fourier transformed to generate a surrogate time series. The randomization ensures that any phase coupling, and thus signs of nonlinearity, is destroyed in the surrogates.

3. The Strategy to Develop the Market

In general, a successful privatization program requires institutional changes that contribute significantly to the strengthening of the legal framework underlying equity investment. However, private control and policy reforms must be maintained during any political backlash. As a consequence, actual progress of privatization builds up confidence over time and this will lead to market deepening, investment and trading. This may explain why privatization may be contemporaneous or even precede successful stock market development. Alternative benefits of successful privatization are improved risk sharing and increased liquidity and activity of the market [24, 28, 29]. One of the main methods to develop privatization, is entering a new stock to the markets for arising competition. But attention to the capability of the markets to accept a new stock is substantial. Without considering the above statement, it is possible to reduce the market's efficiency. In other words, introduction of a new stock to the market usually decreases the stage of development and activity and increases the risk. It has been shown that inefficient markets' stage of development and activity are lower and their risk is higher than efficient markets [28, 29, 39].

The reason why, in very efficient markets of equities and currency exchanges correlations of returns are extremely small, is because any significant correlation would lead to an arbitrage opportunity that is rapidly exploited and thus washed out. Indeed, the fact that

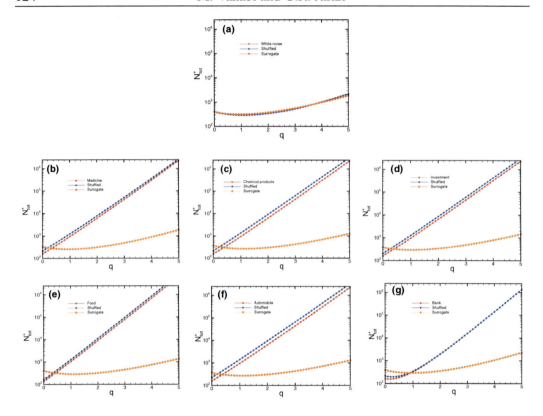

Figure 8. Comparison of generalized total number of Level Crossings with positive slope $N_{tot}^{+}(q)$ of (a) White noise, (b) Medicine, (c) Chemical products, (d) Investment, (e) Food, (f) Automobile and (g) Bank with their shuffled and surrogate.

there are almost no correlations between price variations in efficient markets can be understood from simple calculation [3, 40]. In other words, liquidity and efficiency of markets control the degree of correlation, that is compatible with a near absence of arbitrage opportunity. It is important to consider that, the more intelligent and hard working the investors, the more random is the sequence of price changes generated by such a market.

In the following subsections we try to explain more about activity, stage of development, risk and waiting times which can characterize the market and should be considered before privatization.

3.1. Activity

One of the parameters that should be considered before privatization is activity. When there is no sell and buy in the market, the prices are fixed without any fluctuation. One should pay attention that fluctuation is calculated with respect to the trading volume. With increasing the trading volume, the fluctuation decreases. Indeed, fluctuation is the sign of existence of sell and buy that is called activity [29]. High fluctuation could also increase the risk. The process of buy and sell or activity is a positive parameter which could be effective in determining the real price of the stock and in correctly distributing the wealth. It is obvious that by increasing activity, liquidity increases which can stimulate investors to enter their short-term investment to the market that can again increase (improve) activity. The liquidity of a product can be measured as how often it is bought and sold. Liquidity is characterized by a high level of trading activity.

3.2. Stage of Development

Based on recent research for characterizing the stage of development of markets [25, 29, 26, 27], it is shown that the Hurst exponent (H) has sensitivity to the degree of development of the market. In liquid markets, correlations of returns are small because existence of any information in the market would lead the investors to get use of it and thus washed out. In contrast, if there is no correlation between price variations or if markets are perfectly efficient, the return on gathering information is nil. Therefore, there would be little reason to trade and markets would eventually collapse [41].

One of the important points in market development, is acceptability of the market development by investors. In emerging markets, there exist correlations and information (high value of Hurst exponent) which can stimulate the investors to gain benefits. If the development is accepted by investors, it will be a successful program. In this case, the market parameters improve (higher activity and stage of development and lower risk). In most developing countries and even in some developed countries, "they privatize just for privatization" and not for promoting efficiency, improving the operations of markets, reduction in public debt, etc and in this case there will occur an unsuccessful privatization. This happens because they have not enough attention to the above point and so these markets have not the capability of accepting the new stocks and the development of privatization. This suggests that by considering the current situation, the rate of development and privatization should be controlled. Here, we could ask a question: why the investors do not get use of the present information besides the development?

A: Lack of "liquid investment": This means that the worth of the introduced stocks is more than the worth of the liquid investment. In this case liquidity of the stocks decreases. In other words, exchange of the stocks is reduced and so the liquidity of the market falls and there will be an inefficient and frozen market. In this case privatization is not a successful program for development of the market. In other words, before privatization, attention to the worth of the introduced stocks in comparison with the liquid investment is necessary.

B: Lack of financial security and high risk: This factor ruins the motives of investors for investment. This is one of the main problems in developing countries.

C: "Frozen investment": In some countries, there is not enough study or proper management program for privatization and instead of using privatization for the use of potential intelligence and investment, they privatize for privatization. For example, consider the case that government distribute some stocks between people who did not want to be investors on their own. Hence they do not participate in the exchange of stocks and currency and they form the "frozen investment". Thus they cannot increase the intelligence. These are the stocks that were frozen under the name of the government and now only the name is changed. While the aim of privatization is not the apparent change of the names of the investors.

Thus, for a successful privatization program these three parameters should also be considered. We intend to study development of the market from this aspect by using Level

Crossing analysis.

LC with the power of correlation detection, is a useful tool to find the stage of development of markets [28, 29]. It is known that inefficient markets have long-range correlation. This sensitivity of LC to the market conditions provides a new and simple way of empirically characterizing the development of financial markets. This means that, in mature markets the total positive slope crossings, N_{tot}^+ is fixed or decreases under shuffling effectively, while in emerging markets, it is increased. Recently, many works have focused on the stage of development of the market [26, 27, 25, 28, 29, 42]. As far as stock markets are concerned, the Hurst exponents show remarkable differences between developed and emerging markets. Di Matteo et al (2003) and (2005) found that the emerging markets have $H > 0.5$ whereas the developed ones have $H \leq 0.5$ [26, 27, 25].

3.3. Risk

Nowadays, the importance of risk is clear for everyone. As many researches have shown, many financial crisis such as Asian crisis during 1997-1998 have been related to the lack of suitable risk management. Indeed, risk is one of the important subjects that has been considered by most of the financial organizations e.g. banks, assurance companies etc. In other words, precise recognition of the financial markets and the means to maintain the stability in these markets, is one of the crucial ways to preserve the economic growth of the country. Risk management is one of the main tools for stability of financial markets. In fact, market risk is resulted from the high fluctuation (low frequency regime) in the prices of assets. Assets could be in the form of cash, stocks, lands, gold etc. All of these could have fluctuation in their prices and this is the main result to produce risk. Thus, assessing and pricing the risk properly is of substantial importance. Financial and credit risks [43, 44, 45, 46] play the main roles in bankruptcy of the financial markets. These continuous crisis due to the financial risk have better shown the necessity of attention to the management of risk.

In fact, most of the common methods for risk measurement is based on Value at Risk (VaR) [43, 44, 45]. VaR is a downside risk measure, meaning that it typically focuses on losses. Most of the common methods (ARCH models, variance-covariance, riskmetrics ...) are based on variance and the kinds of it. We want to look at risk from another point of view because of its importance. In fact, small fluctuation in the return of the prices have contribution in the variance and so in risk. But we mention that small fluctuation demonstrate the activity of the market which is a positive parameter. In a market with no buy and sell there is no fluctuation in the price. In this case the variance is zero and there is no risk. It means that we should consider more contribution from larger fluctuation. But we should pay attention to the point that risk is not a totally negative concept. Although the investors could hold their money in the banks without risk, they prefer to invest it in the markets that could have risk. This operation depends on the risk that an investor will take and this is due to two main factors: 1) The worth of his investment and 2) Human psychology. Indeed, in average, the more his investment, the more risk he will take. One of the market factors is knowledge of distribution of the investors and their investment. It is clear that human psychology is important and this is related to social sciences.

3.4. Investment Horizons

To speak about other aspects of the development of markets, we can mention investment horizons. By investment horizons we mean the expectation time for a specified benefit. The quantitative method that is used is inverse statistics which was introduced by Johansen et al [47, 48, 49]. This method has been formed by the main idea that the current prices are the results of the future expectation. In other words, in response to the question of "how to price in the available information?" for the case of a stock, one must consider how the available information affects future earnings of the company. This introduces some ambiguity as not only do peoples expectations to a largely unpredictable future differ, but so do their strategies. But how we can quantify the peoples expectations? One of the important parameters that affect peoples expectations is the expectation time which is defined as the specified time interval that one should wait for a specific change in the price value. The answer to this question can adjust the investors expectations with respect to for example investment horizons. This expectation time can help the investors to invest their money by considering the risk they can take and the fact that how long they intend to hold their investment before taking any profit. The risk that people are willing to take is a subject of the human psychology and social sciences. This can suggest that economics and financial problems are coupled with human sciences.

4. Application

To study the market development, we have analyzed some selected TEPIX subgroup indices using Level Crossing analysis (Fig. 2). These indices are Bank, Medicine, Food, Automobile, Investment, Chemical products. The data are taken from Tehran Securities Exchange Technology Management Company (TSETMC) [50]. Log return time series, $r(t)$ of them from the same time interval: 3 January 2005 to 1 March 2008 have been analyzed. Data have been recorded at each trading day. In addition, we have compared the results with a white noise as a standard reference.

According to Eq. 10 Level Crossing, ν_α^+, is calculated for the indices. Figure 3 shows a comparison of ν_α^+ for TEPIX subgroups as a function of level α. It is clear that ν_α^+ scales inversely with time, so $\tau(\alpha) = \frac{1}{\nu_\alpha^+}$ is a waiting time which the level α will be observed again. Figure 4 shows a comparison of $\tau(\alpha)$ for TEPIX subgroups. These figures show that the behavior of various indices is different.

Table 1 shows the waiting time for meeting various levels from high frequency to low frequency (tails) regimes: $(\tau(\alpha = 0))$ which is the mean of the levels, $(\tau(\alpha = \pm 0.005)$, $\tau(\alpha = \pm 0.01)$ and $\tau(\alpha = \pm 0.02)$ for all selected indices of TEPIX subgroups. The time interval $\tau(\alpha = 0)$ of Bank index is the largest (8.53) and the time interval $\tau(\alpha = 0)$ of Food index is the smallest (5.95) days which are in the same order. This means that in average, it takes more time for meeting the mean of the levels with positive slope for Bank index than Food index. In other words, the Food index lives more in the level $\alpha = 0$. As it is seen in the table 1, there exists an asymmetric behavior when we are moving towards the tails (high levels) and this behavior is in such a way that there is a tendency towards the mean, except the index of Medicine. In all indices except Medicine index, the waiting time interval of right is larger than left tails. This means that when we are in the levels larger than mean we should wait more time for meeting this level with positive slope, than for the same opposite level. According to table 1, in average, the waiting time interval in the tails for Bank index is the smallest, which means that it is financially motivated to absorb capital in this index.

The area under the curves of ν_α^+ shows the total positive Level Crossings, N_{tot}^+ which represents the activity of the market. As it is seen in table 2, Food index has the smallest activity (138.17) and Bank index has the largest one (164.28). This should be noted that the values of the N_{tot}^+ are reported for this time scale (3 Jan. 2005 to 1 Mar. 2008). As it is reported in table 1, the waiting time of the Bank index is the smallest in various levels which means it is more active. Activity or the process of buy and sell is a positive parameter which could be effective in determining the real price of the stock and in correctly distributing the wealth. By increasing activity, liquidity increases.

Figures 5 and 6 show typical comparison of the positive Level Crossings and waiting times of an index (Bank index) and white noise with their shuffled and surrogate, respectively. In order to better compare the results, standard deviation of the white noise is chosen to be the same as the Bank index. It should be noted that, in these figures the standard deviation of the shuffled and surrogate are kept the same as the original ones. Considering that, for a white noise, the Level Crossing curves do not change after shuffling and surrogating processes, any deviation from this behavior shows existence of statistical information and departure from the white noise. As it is seen in figure 5(a), when we are shuffling and surrogating the returns of Bank index, the Level Crossing curve changes. Hence, the area under the curves of the original and its shuffled and surrogate differs. As it is reported in table 2, N_{tot}^+, N_{sh}^+ and N_{su}^+ of the Bank index are 164.28, 218.31 and 389.83, respectively. As it is seen in figure 6, the waiting time for the Bank index and its shuffled and surrogate are shown. The waiting time for the surrogate of the Bank index grows much slower than the original and the shuffled series. This represents that the Bank index is far from the Gaussian function. This shows the existence of risk that will be studied later in this section. As it is seen in the figures 5 and 6, the difference between the surrogate of Bank index and white noise is much smaller than the difference between the shuffled Bank index and the white noise which lead us to the conclusion that the contribution from the PDF is larger than the contribution from the correlation. This is because the index is fat-tailed. This behavior is in good agreement with the results of the table 2. As it is reported in this table, comparison between the relative differences for the Bank index ($|N_{sh}^+ - N_{tot}^+|/N_{tot}^+$ and $|N_{su}^+ - N_{tot}^+|/N_{tot}^+$ which are 0.33 and 1.37 respectively) will reveal that the contribution from the PDF is larger. The results of other indices are listed for better comparison.

Since activity, $N_{tot}^+(q = 0)$ is very sensitive to correlation, it changes when the time series is shuffled so that the correlation disappears. When the relative difference of the shuffled and the original series, $|N_{sh}^+ - N_{tot}^+|/N_{tot}^+$ is positive, the series is correlated and when this relative difference is negative, the series is anti-correlated. This behavior may not be seen when calculated directly by standard models. One of the advantages of Level Crossing method is that no scaling feature is explicitly required. Thus, by comparing the difference between $N_{tot}^+(q = 0)$ and $N_{sh}^+(q = 0)$ (after shuffling), the stage of development of markets can be determined. Smaller relative difference denotes larger stage of development. The results of this relative difference is listed in table 2, which the minimum is 0.19 for Food index and the maximum is 0.38 for the Automobile index. These results show that the Medicine index is the index with highest stage of development and the stage of development of Automobile index is the lowest.

Also, activity, $N_{tot}^+(q = 0)$, is sensitive to deviation of PDF from normal distribution. Thus, it changes when the time series is surrogated so that the PDF changes to a Gaussian one. When the relative difference of the surrogate and the original series, $|N_{su}^+ - N_{tot}^+|/N_{tot}^+$ is positive, the series is fat-tailed and when this relative difference is negative, Gaussian distribution is wider than the series. Thus, by comparing the difference between $N_{tot}^+(q = 0)$ and $N_{su}^+(q = 0)$ (after surrogating), the contribution of sudden changes in activity can be determined. Larger relative difference denotes larger risk. The results of this relative difference is listed in table 2, which the minimum is 339.56 for Medicine index and the maximum is 408.60 for the Food index. All the relative changes are positive which means that all the indices are fat-tailed. Fat tails of a distribution refers to a much larger probability for large price changes than what is to be expected from the random walk or Gaussian hypothesis and they imply additional risk.

For a better comparison, Hurst exponent which was obtained by using the detrended fluctuation analysis (DFA) method [51, 52], are reported in table 2 too. As it is seen they are in agreement with the results of the Level Crossing method. But it should be noted that errors in evaluating the exponent is more. Inefficient markets are associated with high value of Hurst exponent and developed markets are associated with low value of the exponent. In particular, it is found that all emerging markets have Hurst exponents larger than 0.5 (strongly correlated) whereas all the developed markets have Hurst exponents near to or less than 0.5 (white noise or anti-correlated). As reported [26, 25, 28], at one end of the spectrum, there are stocks like Nasdaq 100 (US), $S\&P500$ (US), Nikkei 225 (Japan) and so on. Whereas, at the other end, there are TEPIX, the Indonesian JSXC, the Peruvian LSEG, etc. We notice that TEPIX belong to the emerging markets category and it is far from an efficient and developed market.

When we apply Eq. 13 for small q regime, high frequency events ($\alpha = 0$) are more significant, whereas in the large q regime, low frequency (the tails) is more significant. Figure 7 compares the generalized total number of positive slopes Level Crossings, $N_{tot}^+(q)$ of different indices and a white noise. In this figure, for better comparison, we choose the same variance for all of them. As it is seen in the figure, $N_{tot}^+(q)$ for the Bank index is below the other indices for $q \gg 1$ and the Food index is above them. This means that in these indices, Food index is higher in risk and Bank is lower. This figure shows how $N_{tot}^+(q)$ for the indices are deviated from a white noise. To know the reason of this deviation we compare the behavior of $N_{tot}^+(q)$ for each index with its shuffled and surrogate in figure 8. White noise behavior has been plotted for a better decision. It is clear that $N_{tot}^+(q)$ of white noise and its shuffled and surrogate have the same behavior because a white noise is an uncorrelated series with normal distribution. The surrogated $N_{tot}^+(q)$ for all the indices shows little difference from the white noise. This means that PDF leads this deviation in our indices. $N_{tot}^+(q)$ for the moments $q \gg 1$ is sensitive to the tail of events which is the sudden changes. As it is shown in the figure for $q \gg 1$, the largest difference between $N_{tot}^+(q)$ for the original and the surrogate series is for Food index and the smallest difference is for the Bank index. This means that Food index is more risky than other indices and the risk of the Bank index is the smallest. Another point that should be noted, is that while for $q < 1$, $N_{tot}^+(q)$ is different for Bank index and its shuffled, this difference could not be seen for $q \gg 1$.

Table 1. The values of waiting time, $\tau(\alpha)$ for different levels, α for some TEPIX subgroup indices.

Index	$\tau(\alpha=0)$	$\tau(\alpha=-0.005)$	$\tau(\alpha=0.005)$	$\tau(\alpha=-0.01)$	$\tau(\alpha=0.01)$	$\tau(\alpha=-0.02)$	$\tau(\alpha=0.02)$
Bank	8.53	9.38	11.24	15.39	21.45	32.18	54.46
Medicine	7.87	22.47	31.47	78.68	64.35	353.98	236.02
Chemical products	7.61	11.42	14.45	29.50	59.00	88.50	101.14
Automobile	7.30	16.09	19.14	35.40	47.19	70.80	176.99
Investment	6.74	15.73	30.78	33.70	78.68	56.64	236.02
Food	5.95	20.23	44.27	37.26	101.11	64.36	236.02

Table 2. The values of total number of crossings with positive slope for some TEPIX subgroup indices, $N_{tot}^+(q=0)$ (activity), their shuffled, surrogate, their relative differences between original data & their shuffled (stage of development) and surrogate (deviation from a normal distribution) and comparison of them with Hurst exponents.

Index	N_{tot}^+	N_{sh}^+	N_{su}^+	$\lvert N_{sh}^+ - N_{tot}^+ \rvert / N_{tot}^+$	$\lvert N_{su}^+ - N_{tot}^+ \rvert / N_{tot}^+$	H
Automobile	157.60	217.85	374.19	0.38	1.37	0.71 ± 0.02
Medicine	162.57	222.49	339.56	0.37	1.09	0.64 ± 0.02
Bank	164.28	218.31	389.83	0.33	1.37	0.61 ± 0.02
Chemical products	163.89	212.61	385.44	0.30	1.35	0.60 ± 0.02
Investment	158.87	203.67	390.56	0.28	1.46	0.56 ± 0.02
Food	138.17	164.20	408.60	0.19	1.96	0.55 ± 0.02

This shows that the existence of correlation in high frequency regime is more than the low frequency regime.

Considering all of the above discussions and results, we notice that TEPIX and most of its subgroups belong to the emerging markets category and they are far from efficient and developed markets. Tables 1 and 2 compare the properties of these subgroup indices. Knowledge of distribution of the investors and their investment could be important. In general, the stage of development is substantial for developing the market. Higher stage of development means that this market is closer to an efficient market. Thus, the capability to accept a new stock is more. When there exist investors with limited investment (less risk-taking investors) higher activity and lower risk could be more important. The Food index with highest stage of development is closer to an efficient market but with its lower activity and higher risk for its development, we need more risk-taking investors (the more investment one has, the more risk he will take). In contrast, Bank with highest activity and lowest risk has the middle place in the stage of development. Thus, if investors with limited investment exist, these two parameters are more important. Hence, for development and privatization, knowing the distribution of the investors and their investment and also studying the human psychology is necessary.

5. Conclusion

In this chapter, we have studied some concepts, which are important to develop and privatize markets by Level Crossing approach. We have calculated some parameters of indices which are effective parameters in development and privatization of markets. These parameters include: activity, stage of development, risk and investment horizons (which depends on waiting time). The subgroups with higher activity and stage of development and lower risk and appropriate investment horizons (the waiting time interval that one should wait for a specific change in the price value) are more suitable for development and privatization than other subgroups. This method is based on stochastic processes which should grasp the scale dependency of any time series in a most general way. We have applied this method to 6 selected subgroup indices (Bank, Medicine, Food, Automobile, Investment, Chemical products) of Tehran stock market and compared their properties.

References

[1] Joseph McCauley, *Dynamics of Markets, Econophysics and Finance*, Cambridge University Press (Cambridge, 2004)

[2] Rosario N. Mantegna, H. Eugene Stanley, *An Introduction to Econophysics: Correlations and Complexity in Finance*, Cambridge University Press (Cambridge, 1999)

[3] D. Sornette, Why Stock Markets Crash, by Princeton University Press (2003), D. Sornette, *Physics Reports* **378** (2003) 198.

[4] Bertrand Roehner, *Patterns of Speculation - A Study in Observational Econophysics*, Cambridge University Press (Cambridge, 2002)

[5] B. K. Chakrabarti, A. Chakraborti, A. Chatterjee, *Econophysics and Sociophysics : Trends and Perspectives*, Wiley-VCH, Berlin (2006)

[6] Jean-Philippe Bouchaud, Marc Potters, *Theory of Financial Risk and Derivative Pricing*, Cambridge University Press (2003).

[7] Philip Ball, Econophysics: Culture Crash. *Nature* **441**, (2006) 686-688.

[8] E. Samanidou, E. Zschischang, D. Stauffer and T. Lux, *Rep. Prog. Phys.* **70** (2007) 409-450.

[9] Rudolf Friedrich, Joachim Peinke, and Christoph Renner, *Physical Review Letters,* **84**(22), (2000), 52245227; Marcel Ausloos and K. Ivanova, Physical Review E, 68(4), 6122, (2003).

[10] *The challenges of privatization: an international analysis*, Bernardo Bortolotti, D. Siniscalco, Oxford University Press, (2004).

[11] Bernardo Bortolotti, Frank de Jong, Giovanna Nicodano, Ibolya Schindele, *Journal of Banking & Finance* **31** (2007) 297316.

[12] Bernardo Bortolotti, Marcella Fantini and Carlo Scarpa, *International Review of Finance,* **3**:2, (2002) 131-163.

[13] Bernardo Bortolotti, D. Siniscalco and M. Fantini, *Journal of Public Economics,* **88**, (2003) 305-332.

[14] Josef C. Brada, *J. Econ. Persp.*, **10**, (1996), 67-86.

[15] Aidan R. Vining and Anthony E. Boardman., *Pub. Choice.,* **73**, (1992), 205-239.

[16] Andrei. Shleifer, *J. Econ. Persp.,* **12**, (1998), 133-150.

[17] Maxim Boycko, Andrei Shleifer, and Robert W. Vishny., *European Econ. Rev.,* **40**, (1996), 767-774.

[18] J. A. Kay and D. J. Thompson, *Econ. J.,* **96**, (1986), 18-32.

[19] John Vickers and George Yarrow. *J. Econ. Persp.*, **5**, (1991), 111-132.

[20] Matthew R. Bishop and John A. Kay., *World Develop.,* **17**, (1989), 643-657.

[21] Shleifer, Andrei and Robert W. Vishny., *J. Fin.,* **52**, (1997), 737-783.

[22] http://www.ilga.gov/commission/cgfa2006/

[23] William L. Megginson and Jeffry M. Netter, *Journal of Economic Literature*, **84**(22), (2001), 52245227.

[24] Perotti, Enrico and Pieter van Oijen,*J. Int. Money Fin,* (2000).

[25] P. Norouzzadeh, G. R. Jafari, *Physica A* **356** (2005), 609627.

[26] T. Di Matteo, T. Aste, M. M. Dacorogna, *Physica A* **324** (2003) 183-188.

[27] T. Di Matteo, T. Aste and M. M. Dacorogna, *Journal of Banking & Finance* **29/4** (2005), 827-851.

[28] G. R. Jafari, M. S. Movahed, S. M. Fazeli, M. R. Rahimi Tabar, *J. Stat. Mech.,* P06008 (2006).

[29] M. Vahabi, G. R. Jafari, *Physica A* **385** (2007) 583590.

[30] F. Shahbazi, S. Sobhanian, M. Reza Rahimi Tabar, S. Khorram, G. R. Frootan, and H. Zahed, *J. Phys. A* **36**, 2517 (2003).

[31] F. Ghasemi, Muhammad Sahimi, J. Peinke, R. Friedrich, G. Reza Jafari, and M. Reza Rahimi Tabar, *Phys. Rev. E* **75**, 060102(R) (2007).

[32] P. Diaconis and A. Ram, *Michigan Math. J.* **48**,157 (2000).

[33] Thomas Schreiber and Andreas Schmitz, *Physica D* **142** (2000), 346382.

[34] J. Theiler, S. Eubank, A. Longtin, B. Galdrikian, J. D. Farmer, *Physica D* **58** 77 (1992).

[35] J. Theiler, P. S. Linsay, and D. M. Rubin, *Detecting nonlinearity in data with long coherence times*, Time Series Prediction: Forecasting the Future and Understanding the Past, A.S. Weigend and N.A. Gershenfeld, Proc.Vol. XVII, Addison-Wesley, (1993).

[36] J. Theiler, D. Prichard, *Fields Inst. Commun.* **11** (1997), 99-113.

[37] M. S. Movahed, G. R. Jafari, F. Ghasemi, Sohrab Rahvar and M. Reza Rahimi Tabar, *J. Stat. Mech.* (2006) P02003;

[38] G. R. Jafari, P. Pedram and L. Hedayatifar, *J. Stat. Mech.* P04012 (2007).

[39] M. Pagano, *European Economic Review* **37**, (1993) 11011125.

[40] B. M. Roehner and D. Sornette, *Europian physical Jurnal B,* **16** (2000), 729-739.

[41] S. Grosstman and J. E. Stiglitz, *American Economic review* **70** (1980), 393-408.

[42] G. R. Jafari, A. Bahraminasab, P. Norouzzadeh, *International Journal of Modern Physics C* , Vol. 18, No. 7, (2007) 1223 - 1230.

[43] Tapiero Charles , *Risk and Financial Management: Mathematical and Computational Methods*, John Wiley (2004).

[44] Donald R. van Deventer, Kenji Imai and Mark Mesler, *Advanced Financial Risk Management: Tools and Techniques for Integrated Credit Risk and Interest Rate Risk Management*, John Wiley (2004).

[45] James Lam, *Enterprise Risk Management: From Incentives to Controls*, John Wiley (2003).

[46] E. Perotti, P.van Oijen, *Journal of International Money and Finance* **20** (1), (2001) 4369.

[47] I. Simonsen, M. H. Jensen and A. Johansen, *Eur. Phys. J.* **27** (2002) 583.

[48] M. H. Jensen, A. Johansen and I. Simonsen, *Physica A* **234** (2003) 338; M.H. Jensena.

[49] A. Johansen, F. Petroni, I. Simonsen, *Physica A* **340** (2004) 678 684.

[50] www.tsetmc.com

[51] C. K. Peng, S. V. Buldyrev, S. Havlin, M.Simons , H. E. Stanley , and A. L. Goldberger , *Phys. Rev. E* **49**, (1994) 1685-1689.

[52] S. M. Ossadnik, S. B. Buldyrev, A. L. Goldberger, S. Havlin, R. N. Mantegna, C. K. Peng, M. Simons and H. E. Stanley , *Biophys. J.* **67**, 64 (1994).

INDEX

D

J

K

L

M

N

Q

R

S

T

U

V